Excuses Galore

...and why we are prone to make them !

The Fox and the Grapes[1]
The fox, unable to get the grapes,
decided, it is not ripe

Zeb O. Waturuocha
Ph.D

[1] http://en.wikipedia.org/wiki/File:
The_Fox_and_the_Grapes_-_Project_Gutenberg_etext_19994.jpg

F-2/16, Ansari Road, Daryaganj, New Delhi-110002
E-mail: info@unicornbooks.in • Website: www.unicornbooks.in
☎ 011-23275434, 23262683, 23250704

Branch : Mumbai
23-25, Zaoba Wadi, Thakurdwar, Mumbai-400002
☎ 022-22010941, 022-22053387
E-mail: rapidex@bom5.vsnl.net.in

ISBN: 978-81-7806-333-1
Excuses Galore

Edition: 2014

Printed at : *Unique Color Carton, Mayapuri, New Delhi-110064*

Contents

Part-III : Interpersonal Effects of Excuses

Part-IV : Work Effect of Excuses

Preface

The idea of writing a book on Excuses is not to exonerate myself from this self-defeating behaviour. The idea is to call the attention of the reader to take a profound look and consider the devastating effect of setting up 'Excuses' as a tool in life's journey. Do you recollect the various occasions wherein you have availed of Excuses to stay in control, to win favour, to exempt yourself from blame?

Whatever happens, whoever and whatever you are, you have used Excuse in your life. You surely got what you wanted - but is your conscience free? Have you continued to use excuse consciously, or has excuse become a way of life for you? Has Excuse come to stay in your way of life synonymous with Reason ?

This book is written in order that you may find answer to the above questions? There are different types of excuses and there are different reasons for using excuses. Sometimes, excuses are used to deceive and at other times it is used to save one's face. Many a time excuses are used to buy time and at other times they are resorted to as play things. Whatever be the reason for excuses, there is invariably the opposite of it 'truth' lying somewhere. The challenge is to understand and own why one should use excuses, rather than the truth.

Acknowledgments

In writing this book, I realise that I am not alone in both thought and writing. Essentially, many people have been part of this journey. Maria, Adanna, Uchenna and Ikenna have been the sources of inspiration for all that I think or do and their support is unbounded. I immensely thank Snigdha Patnaik, PhD., and T.T Shrinath, PhD. for their kind words in writing the forward to this book.

In an attempt to sense the mood of readers of this book, I had taken readers' comments from several people and I use this opportunity to thank all of them. A great motivator for writing this book is Suva Chattopadhyay, General Manager, Sales Excellence, Abbott Truecare Pharma Pvt Ltd. A true friend of goodwill and wishes, thank you so much Suva.

I thank my colleague Jenny Davis who not only helped in typing the manuscript but also asked mind-bogging questions that led to deeper search for answers.

I thank Dr. Ashok and all at Unicorn Publishers who have worked hard to give shape to this book by accepting to publish the same.

About the book

This book is fundamentally about the excuses that we make in our everyday lives. You will read and understand the meaning of excuses in its various forms and sources, difference between excuses and reasons as also various types of excuses. You will also read about why people use Excuses and probably compare them with your own reasons for using excuses.

The objective of the book is not to prescribe norms for excuses or reasons, but for the reader to become aware of the fact that excuses are distinct from reasons, and that excuses impact every aspect of our lives. Excuses have become part of our daily lives that we become oblivious of their effect on our personal, professional and social lives, and our personal effectiveness and relationships. If this awareness is brought home to the reader, then he/she has a choice to continue to use "excuses" as reason or decide to use "reason" rather than excuses.

The book opens with forward written by two dear friends who have found no fault in whatever I do even if it is an excuse, they accept me as I am.

This is followed with a poem that says it all "It is difficult but challenging" which tends to explain why excuses are difficult to avoid because others are doing it. Who would dare to be different?

The Book is divided into Parts as follows:

Part I - Introductory

The introductory section has three chapters.

Chapter 1 reiterates the words of Gordon Lawrence which states that "Much of the stuff of the social arrangements human beings make to organise their social life is to defend themselves against psychotic anxieties."

Chapter 2 discusses the learning of behaviour and how behaviour is modified. It also discusses how the meaning making process is responsible for the decisions we accord and that this meaning making process is influenced by the learning of behaviour.

In **chapter 3**, attempt has been made to describe and define Excuses to an understandable extent, along with the various sources and types of Excuses. The chapter also talks about why people use Excuses.

Excuses Vs Reason : The chapter markedly distinguishes between Excuses and Reason to ensure that the reader understands the difference between these two terms. The reader stops using these two terms synonymously as if he/she was ignorant of the difference.

Excuses Vs Lies : In this chapter, the author brings out the marked distinction between an excuse and a lie. He defines excuse as something that can be true or untrue but finds 'lie' as absolutely untrue in whichever way it is viewed. He also discusses some of the ill-effects of lies especially in relation to health.

Part II - Intrapersonal Effect of Excuses

There are three chapters in this part and each chapter discusses what Excuses does to the individual that uses excuses to get what he/she wants.

Chapter 4 is about Excuses and Dissonance : Cognitive dissonance is a discomfort caused by holding conflicting cognitions - the internal turmoil of the individual who offers Excuse as Reason.

Chapter 5 Excuses and Emotions : Reviews the emotional state of both the giver and receiver of Excuses. Emotional intelligence is the ability to recognize, understand and use feelings to improve relationships. How does excuse affect emotional relationship between people?

Chapter 6 Excuses and Goal Achievement : Everybody works with written and/or unwritten goal in mind that drives every action. Even excuse is an action driven by goal. In this chapter, the reader will understand the impact of excuses on goal achievement either of his/her own or those of others.

Excuses and Responsibility : Excuse is the easiest way to shirk responsibility. Who is responsible for this poor result? This person is to be blamed. In other words, excuses, shirking responsibility and blame go hand in hand. This chapter reviews what happens when the individual shirks responsibility as synonymous with shirking power.

Part III - Interpersonal Effect of Excuses

Chapter 7 Excuses and Relationship : Life is about relationship. Excuse makers risk being seen as deceptive, self-absorbed, and ineffectual; they are viewed as unreliable social participants with flawed character. This chapter reviews how excuses can ruin relationship, an essential pre-requisite for human existence and survival.

Chapter 8 Excuses and Personal Effectiveness : Personal effectiveness has three dimensions - self disclosure, openness and perceptiveness. Chapter 8 discusses how excuse impacts this core being of effectiveness.

Chapter 9 Excuses and Decision Making : Man's life is full of decision making from the decision to get up from bed in the morning to the decision to do anything until retirement thereto. In Chapter 9, we review the impact of excuses on the various decisions that we are called upon to make in different capacities.

Excuses and Trust : This chapter reviews the meaning of trust and its critical role in our lives. It goes on to scrutinize the word TRUST as an acronym for the factors contributing to an effective life.

Part IV - Work Effect of Excuses

Chapter 10 Excuses and Team work : The time has come when one man can neither manage an organisation nor produce all that organisation stands for without the cooperation of all stake holders including employees. Chapter 10 takes a look at Team work or team effectiveness and the impact of excuses on the bottom line of team effectiveness.

Chapter 11 Excuses and Leadership : There is no leader without followers. A leader is one who gets others to do what they would not ordinarily do and that is why leadership is more endowed with character than position. To be an effective leader, one has to be a model for one's followers, there is no doubt that a leader who uses excuses to lead his people will not be successful. **Chapter 11** reviews how Excuses impact effective leadership.

Excuses and Commitment : This chapter defines commitment and how it drives the efforts dedicated to achieve objectives. It argues that Commitment is a strong force to be reckoned with, which does not allow Excuses to surface and impact performance.

Foreword-I

As I stared at my computer screen wondering what to write, I kept thinking of what 'NOT making excuses' meant to me, and I was reminded of a quote from Mary Anne Radmacher which goes

"I am the owner of my choices.

I am the source for the perspectives
I choose to hold...

regardless of how aware I am of why or how
I come to possess

that particular perspective.

It takes courage to look into the mirror of our souls,
absent excuses."

Making excuses is a choice that I make, whether it is borne out of any conscious or unconscious action. And so of course, not making the excuse is about taking responsibility for the choices that I make. It takes guts, gumption, and the ability to stand naked in front of myself and glory in being me.

I loved reading the book, kept reflecting on all the excuses that I make, as I go through life. Don't all of us do? I also got in touch with my own journey to be the real me. To gather slowly and painfully the courage to be authentic and honest, and not utter the excuse that oftentimes lie at the tip of my tongue, almost like a diver about to leap off the diving board. And then face the music for telling the truth! However, the music has not always been painful and a cacophony. It's an ongoing and wonder-some path and the payoffs have been amazing. I have been surprised at the other person's willingness to accept me, for being me, and appreciate my honesty. I have been struck by how far the fear that makes me utter the excuse is often illusory, and that reality can be so different.

The situations and examples in the book were all so familiar, and I went through the whole gamut of emotions as I went on reading. I felt sheepish, embarrassed, and thoughtful, amused at myself, sad and reflective, and as I connected with what Zeb has written. It also helped me understand some parts of why I do what I do. I am someone who needs to understand before I can change, and the book helped me a great deal understand myself. It made the path of my own voyage of getting to the real, authentic me a little more clear.

'Excuses' is a wonderful book that I am sure will enlighten, fascinate, help in reflection and be a companion in your own growth path. It does not tender any advice, but, nevertheless, helps you understand your actions with transparency and learn of the motives attributed to them. The choice you make in moving forward is entirely up to you. I liked being shown a way forward and exercising the freedom of choosing what to do, rather than being prescribed a road to follow.

Zeb is a dear friend who I have known for over a decade now. We began as co-travelers in learning spaces, and have grown to become colleagues and collaborators in different ways. I love his profound insights and deep thoughts, his authenticity and integrity, and his quirky sense of humour that emerges at unexpected moments and lights up everything around. I wish him and this book success, and a wonderful open audience, who will read it with their mind and their heart.

Snigdha Pattnaik, Ph.D.
Faculty, OB & HRM,
Xavier Institute of Management, Bhubaneswar

Forward-II

Zeb O Waturuocha's latest offering 'Excuses,' clearly emphasise the manifold ways in which we take a self deceptive. Although excuse has much to do with my sense of self-preservation, yet this is only in the short run. When I give an excuse, while the assumed belief is relief, I am soon overwhelmed by both guilt and shame concurrently. If these feelings of guilt and shame when left unattended to, soon consume my sense of well being.

When I give an excuse, I betray my sense. Thus, instead of viewing the other person as one like me, I view him or her as an object; I manipulate, discount and devalue. However, excuses, I must acknowledge, are a terrific way of coping; they let me off the hook and help me justify.

The Arbinger Institute which has done much work on self-deception says that justification, rationalization and fault finding are ways to dull ourselves to live in 'maya' or 'illusion.' Reality is distorted and thus corrupts my world through this distortion. Excuses are no different; they are intelligent ways of denying the truth and thus breeding a 'lie' in me.

Zeb's book is more than a mere self-help book. It is indeed a book on self-empowerment. It is well researched and substantiates knowledge with erudition and scholarship.

I recommend this book, when it is published, and urge people to acquire one, read it, digest it and practise the suggestions offered. It is particularly useful for leaders who have constantly to battle average and poor performance; explained away by people through reason. Leaders can tell those they lead that excuses not only demean the purveyor of the excuse but also those who listen to them.

Srinath, T.T. Ph.D.
Certified Trainer in Applied Behavioural Sciences
Chennai

It is Difficult But Challenging[2]

To Appreciate : When others are criticizing

To Build : When others are destroying

To Co-operate : When others are resisting

To Decide : When others are misguiding

To Expedite : When others are delaying

To Forgive : When others are revenging

To Give : When others are refusing

To Help : When others are promising

To Ignore : When others are condemning

To Justify : When others are disputing

To be Kind : When others are cursing

To Lead : When others are confusing

To Motivate : When others are discouraging

To Neglect : When others are disturbing

To Oblige : When others are hesitating

To Participate : When others are avoiding

To Question : When others are dictating

To Respect : When others are complaining

To Serve : When others are despairing

To Think over : When others are advising

To Unite : When others are dispersing

To Verify : When others are doubting

To Work : When others are postponing

To Xerox truth : When others are hiding

To Yield no hatred : When others are harming

To Zeal & Console : When others are depressing.

Anonymous

---

[2]http://topworldrecords.blogspot.in/2005_12_01_archive.html

Part-I

Prelude

Excuses are the nails used to build a house of failure

—Don Wilder and Bill Rechin

What devastating emotional disease has plagued humankind throughout recorded history, since the dawn of social awareness? The awakening answer is: low self-esteem. Quite simply, the vast majority of society suffers from the emotionally crippling disease known as low self-esteem. The *low self-esteem syndrome* has been unintentionally passed from parent to child, teacher to child, generation to generation, since the beginning of civilization. Almost everyone you know or meet suffers from some form of low self-esteem. This is true because no one wants to be different, no one wants to be seen as an island, the need to belong, to be part of, to be owned, respected and honoured is so pressing.

How often do you do or say something that does not appeal to you, yet you find justification for the action or the talk?

How many times do you walk out of your value and ethical standards, yet pretend to think that you are right?

How often do you violate your own principles and practices but never felt embarrassed, rather find explanations for what you did?

How often do you attack others in relationship even before they make their intentions known?

How many times have you postponed things that need immediate attention by assigning excuses as reasons?

What purpose does it serve to find justification for what we think is not right or proper?

In his article, the presence of totalitarian states-of-mind in institutions, W. Gordon Lawrence, writes:

"Much of the stuff of the social arrangements human beings make to organise their social life is to defend themselves against psychotic anxieties - the fear of annihilation, the fear of being made a nothing, the fear of not being able to make sense of what realities may be, the fear of disorder and chaos, the fear of disintegration, the fear of loss, ending and death. These fears are acutely present in psychic life during earliest infancy and can be reactivated at any time in our subsequent lives when the circumstances constrain them."[3]

Robert Young has written that 'much if not most of our group behaviour and institutional arrangements, are quite specifically and exquisitely designed to avoid consciously experiencing psychotic anxiety. Moreover, the psychotic processes are in danger of breaking through from moment to moment.'[4]

Young continued that, "Humans come to their roles with their personal psychic history. Given the nature of the changing, turbulent, global, commercial environment which generates anxiety and fear, managers are often pressed into only being able to interpret reality from the paranoid-schizoid position. This, if you will, is the mental set which is mobilised. The paranoid schizoid position is one in which '...anxieties of a primitive nature threaten the immature ego and lead to a mobilisation of primitive defences. Splitting, idealisation and projective identification operate to create rudimentary structures made up of idealised good objects kept far apart from the persecutory bad ones.[5] The individual impulses are similarly split and he directs all his love towards the good object and all his hatred against the bad one.[6]

❏❏❏

---

[3]W. Gordon Lawrence, MA, Dr rer oec. THE PRESENCE OF PSYCHOTIC ANXIETIES IN INSTITUTIONS - http://human-nature.com/free-associations/lawren.html

[4]Young, Robert (1994) MENTAL SPACE. Process Press, London

[5]MELANIE KLEIN I by Robert M. Young - http://www.human-nature.com/rmyoung/papers/pap127h.html

[6]Steiner, John (1987) The Interplay between Pathological Organisation and the Paranoid-Schizoid and Depressive Positions. INT. J. PSYCHO-ANAL., 68: 69-80.

The Learning of Behaviour

We live in the most rapidly changing and complex environment that ever existed. To meet up with the compulsions of our daily and many complex social judgments, we almost always tend to rely on learned and automatic responses. Obviously, no one person has the knowledge and expertise to deal with varying decision issues that arise in our daily transactions. What we observe is that we allow our behaviour to be influenced at times by others and by what is happening around us. As social creatures-born dependent on others, living our lives, interacting with others, we are prepared for group living by learning the language, demeanour, beliefs, attitudes, cultural norms, and social values of those around us. We learn adaptation consciously or unconsciously. Social behaviour reflects both conscious and unconscious learning, presumably through Observation learning (modelling), in which we watch others behaviour and then copy.

Classical conditioning, (Pavlovian; respondent) in which the pairing of a conditioned stimulus (bell) with an unconditioned stimulus (meat powder) elicits an unconditioned response (salivation). Repetition produces a conditioned reflex in which the bell alone elicits the salivation.

Operant conditioning, (Skinnerian; instrumental) where learning occurs as a consequence of reinforcement. (If response is reinforced, its frequency will increase; if it is punished, its frequency will decrease.)

Cognitive social learning: *i.e.* thoughts, feelings, images, and memories — the person's inner experiences are crucial factors in learning.[7]

In recent times, theories of learning have become more interactive, seeming acquired or inherited behaviour, internal cognitive factors, and environmental influences operating as reciprocal determinants of each other (i.e. behaviour affects the environment and cognitions; cognitions affect the environment and behaviour; and the environment influences behaviour and cognitions).

---

[7]NEW - Eulogy to Margaret Singer-Group Psychodynamics and CULTS– THE MERCK MANUAL OF DIAGNOSIS AND THERAPY FIFTEENTH EDITION

Modifying Behaviour[8]

Historically, the power of certain persons to dramatically influence others was considered supernatural (i.e. the influencer was a magician or witch with secret potions, and arcane knowledge. Some people have, in most cases, attained compliance and influence through coercion, brutality or the wielding of religious, political, or financial power.

All these are done to persuade the other person to believe, do, behave, accept....consider what the person would not have ordinarily given a dam about. The Wikipedia defines Persuasion as a process aimed at changing a person's (or a group's) attitude or behaviour toward some event, idea, object, or other person(s), by using written or spoken words to convey information, feelings, or reasoning, or a combination thereof. This free online dictionary describes persuasion as underneath the umbrella term of Influence.

While there are varying methods of persuasion or "make believe", the most commonly used are "excuses" which does not cause the reporting person to show evidence nor does it provide the receiver the tools for verification. Another quality of this technique of persuasion is that the persuader is able to keep his subject unaware of his/her intention to convince and to

[8]Adapted from: THE MERCK MANUAL OF DIAGNOSIS AND THERAPY - Readers Digest/December 1, 2003

bring his subject to his side without the others knowledge.

We are all influenced to some extent by advertising, or find ourselves "going along with the group" without realizing how influenced we are by merely being in a crowd (e.g. at a rally or sporting event), or how our behaviour is swayed by emotion caused by the speech of a political orator. Admittedly, there are some persons amongst us with hard mentality.

In general, the people tend to pretend as though they were not influenced or not easily persuaded by others. It appears that such admission signifies weakness or inconsistency or being swerved around. It is our interest to make others believe that our actions are deliberate; we are not persuaded, regulated or directed by others' opinion or ideas. We are completely independent in our thoughts and opinions nothing moves us away from ourselves.

Let us admit that each one of us influences, persuades or misleads others and that, reciprocally, others do the same to us. The difference would be in the degree of resistance that we display, *i.e.*, our vulnerability to follow the persuader. This also would vary from individual to individual and from person to person but depends on the following:-

Timing : If the individual being persuaded is in a hurry, ignorant, unsure, lonely, does not care, uninformed, distracted or tired...

Status and Power : If the individual who is persuading is highly placed in social, economic and political status.

Clarity and Sureness : A person with clarity and sureness, presence of mind, ability to read between lines or to understand what is said from what is not said, insights, ability to intuit, pre-suppose.....

Position : People in complying positions (receive and take instructions) such as high pressure sales persons and representatives who have been trained in the use of influencing techniques

Mankind has devised several ways of warding off the influence of the influencer without sounding deceptive, though he is deceptive in this connection. It is often not easy to counter the expert eyes and methodology of the influencer to the extent that it requires guts to refuse to buy-in to his demands.

One of the methods, and which is mostly by used by many is the method of finding a scapegoat to be held responsible when the demand of the influencer is not met. The scapegoat takes any form or shape but generally termed as "excuse". 'I could not complete this work because I was busy with other things', 'Yes, I visited the client but he was not available', 'I wanted to do it but I was unwell' and so on. Almost every person

---

[9]Divine Protection *www.boreme.com/posting.php?id=27206*

has used these sentences at some point of time or the other in their lives. But what is the reality?[9]

My Meaning-Making Process

Every interaction involves assumption. How real are these assumptions? What do I do if these assumptions prove to be wrong? There is always a pool of information or data available for us to see or not to see, to use or to ignore and using our senses, we become selective and choose mainly those things that do not confront or contradict our belief. The assumptions and interpretations are based on factors such as present state of mind, experience, background, knowledge, socialization etc. It is on the basis of these assumptions that conclusions are made and action taken. This is properly explained by the concept of 'The Ladder of Influence[10]

In other words, the excuses that one provides is based on certain assumption about the situation or the individual to whom the excuse is provided. The process is referred to as climbing the "ladder of inference" and here I intend to use it to explain the meaning making process that every individual follows in every transaction.

---

[10]Source: Concept initially developed by Chris Argyrols, then popularized in **The Fifth Discipline Field book** (1994) by Peter M. Senge, Art Kleiner, Charlotte Roberts, Richard B. Ross, and Bryan J. Smith.

The graphic given below illustrates this concept and how it works:

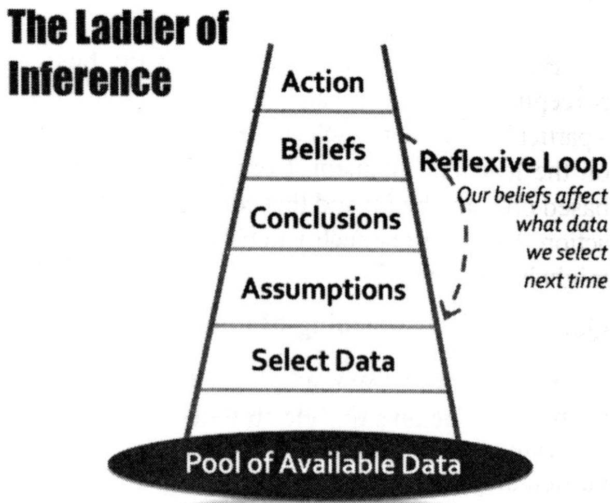

In the pool of available data, note that as transaction (interaction with others) emerge, there are several data available to select from.

For example, your boss reminds you about the target to be achieved and within the given timeframe. This opens a plethora of data before you –

- he thinks that if he does not remind me, I will not remember;
- he thinks I am not doing my work,
- somebody must have told him something about me;

- he just wants to target me,
- he wants to ensure that I meet my target for my own good.......

Based on earlier experience with the boss, self perception in the present and other factors stated earlier, a particular data item is selected and assumption is made on the leaders' comment. Conclusion is then drawn based on some belief and this conclusion reflects into action. Excuse is one such action though the assumption might be unfounded.

Questioning My Meaning-Making Process

If I were more effective through honesty, it would be necessary to question this meaning-making process, especially the assumptions behind the selection of some particular data and not the others. If one is committed to making changes and being authentic, then, one should be ready to confront oneself with such questions as :

- What are the underlying assumptions leading to the conclusion and probable action?
- What experience is driving this assumption or selection of this data, why not other data?
- What justification does one have to state that this is the best and the only right way to act in this given situation?
- What is the role of bias in the conclusion and subsequent action that one has taken?

❑❑❑

What is an Excuse?

Excuses are the tools with which persons with no purpose in view build for themselves great monuments of nothing.

—Steven Grayhm

Excuse is an inferior or inadequate specimen of something specified, usually a well crafted lie and something people subscribe to religiously. Excuse is by default, anything you say after doing something wrong. Excuse is always given for a purpose and this purpose is usually in the minds of the person offering the excuse and this purpose might not be obvious to the receiver of the excuse. Excuses come in the form of an out and out rationalisation or denial of responsibility.

Excuse is a powerful tool in the hands of people to exonerate themselves from blames, disown responsibilities and shirk work not done; as a result excuse is offered in various forms and for various purposes.

Reason	Forgiveness	Plea	Exempt
Justification Pretext Defence Apology Plea Explanation	Pardon Let off Acquit Absolve Tolerate Exonerate	Justify Make allowances for Bear with Tolerate Let off Relieve Spare	Let off Free Release Discharge Spare

But did you Know that Excuses are People at their Creative Best?[11]

Excuses are often made up under the stimulus of impulse and reflex responses. Some people are labouring under the serious misconception that setting up excuses is a trait that calibrates a person's intelligence. The quick witted give good excuses that are usually mistakenly acknowledged by the counter party as 'reasons', and not so witted people give excuses that are seen as dumb and received with frowns and doubts. Excuses can therefore be a measure of how quick witted one is. But, nevertheless, excuses entail ultering lies, thus they constitute sins.

[11]The Butterfly Tales, Tuesday September 15, 2009

The best way to check your wit, therefore, seem to be to look at how good your excuse is, by always gauging it against the intensity of yelling or nagging that follows, since excuses are generally introduced to a conversation when a questioning nag erupts. Good excuses not only quell a torrential nag storm, but if you are really good, you might even get an apology.[12]

Each one of us has been in a situation where he/she was unable to keep a promise or commitment? It may be arriving late to the work place or meeting an appointment time, it may be inability to take a child to the playground, or repayment of loan, it may be late for dinner with your partner or not wanting to be a part of an activity in spite of promising to be counted.

The question is, after you come to know that you cannot deliver, how do you explain why you were unable to meet your obligation to the other party? Do you stand in the truth, own your actions and give an honest reason, or do you externalise the cause or make excuses concerned only with freeing yourself from blame?

When we are unable to deliver, we offer an excuse. The excuse presents an animate or inanimate object as the reason for not performing. If it is an animate object, it has to be a person who is not present at the time of the excuse. The situation presented for blame will never have an opportunity to express its own side of the story.

---

[12]The Butterfly Tales...: Giving Excuses
thebutterflytales.blogspot.com/2009/09/giving-excuses.html

For example, late coming has been blamed on several things including traffic jam, vehicle break down, accident, power failure, child sickness, family issues, and several other things. Where would one go to verify the facts of these stories?

Of course, some of them are verifiable if there is interest to do so and depending on how high the stakes are. But in most cases, people do not need to go further to understand that excuse is being offered to them as reason.

Sources of Excuses

How do people find appropriate excuses that match the situation at hand? In my opinion, excuses are not learned but, as stated earlier, People are able to pre-empt or spontaneously manufacture excuses in the guise of Reasoning. According to Marcus Stroup, *"There aren't nearly enough crutches in the world for all the lame excuses"*. People at their best in the manufacture of excuses tend to employ several ingredients extractable from the alphabets and some of these extractions are noted here.[13]

Abstraction

Abstraction is the process of taking away or removing characteristics from something to reduce it

---

[13]The meanings have been taken from all sources including Wikipedia and websites. Examples are mine and if perchance it matches with an earlier example, should be treated as a coincidence.

to some set of essential characteristics. Absence of mind; pre-occupation - the process of formulating generalized ideas or concepts by extracting common qualities from specific examples - the act of withdrawing or removing. Excuse emanating from abstraction contains a skeletal component of reality hence it is easier to accept the excuse as reason. For example, traffic jam has become a standard excuse when one has no justifiable reason to be late to an appointment.

Branding

Human branding or stigmatizing is the process in which a mark, usually a symbol or ornamental pattern, is burned into the skin of a living person, with the intention that the scar makes it permanent. In the sense used here, it is the process of associating an individual or group of individuals with a particular behaviour.[14] Excuse resulting from branding is often judgmental and can only pass as reason if the person receiving the excuse is also biased about the object of reference. For example, "He does not see reasons but loves excuses."

Carving

While Branding take the form of name calling or association with a person or behaviour, Carving takes the form of giving shape to the individual being perceived. It follows, therefore, the concept of "cast in

[14]en.wikipedia.org/wiki/Human_branding

concrete" to the extent that when the behaviour is changed or modified, the carving does not seem to fade with the changes and, sometimes, the changes are not noticed. The individual is not taken seriously even when reason is offered; the same is taken as excuse. For example, "He is always like that," or "He does not understand."

Deduction

Deduction, is reasoning which constructs or evaluates deductive arguments. Deductive arguments are attempts to show that a conclusion necessarily follows from a set of premises. A deductive argument is valid if the conclusion does follow necessarily from the premises, i.e., if the conclusion must be true provided that the premises are true. A deductive argument is sound if its premises are true.[15] Deductive arguments are valid or invalid, sound or unsound, but are never true or false. For example, "I assumed that you will be late…"

Experience

Experience as a general concept comprises knowledge of, or skill in, or observation of something or some event gained through involvement in or exposure to that thing or event. The history of the word *experience* aligns it closely with the concept of *experiment*. When people use their experience to give an excuse, it is always difficult to argue it out with them. For example, when a person says that in his

[15]www.scribd.com/doc/37836179/Nursing-Theories

10-15 years experience in this organisation or in this field, sales has always experienced nose-dive at this time of the year to explain why the sales man has not performed well in the quarter. It is relatively difficult to argue with him unless you ask for trend map which may or may not prove the fact.

Following

The art of doing something because others are doing the same. How would I look if I do things contrary to what others are doing? I need to fall in line with others, or be damned. How would I comply with when others are giving excuses? For example, "I could not help it as it looked as a trend among...." It is the way things are done here.

Ganging

Coming together for the purpose of supporting or opposing something. Sometimes, excuses are made to support the position taken by others to a supporting or opposing viewpoint or direction. For "let us ensure that we all say that we hold the same opinion...."

Hijacking

Emotional hijacking occurs when you are not aware of you're here-and-now, rather than accept this state of absence in the present, you present excuses as though you were mentally present. For example "I was not aware that the outcome would be so disastrous."

Identification

Identification is a psychological process whereby the subject assimilates an aspect, property, or attribute of the other and is transformed, wholly or partially, after the model the other provides. It is by means of a series of identifications that the personality is constituted and specified. One who follows a particular doctrine will be identified with that doctrine and provide excuses to justify membership or followership of the doctrine. For example, "He is like me..."

Jealousy

Jealousy is an emotion and typically refers to the negative thoughts and feelings of insecurity, fear, and anxiety over an anticipated loss of something that the person values or aspires for, such as a relationship, friendship, promotion or love.[16] Jealousy often consists of a combination of emotions such as anger, sadness, and disgust. Jealousy is among the most common sources of excuse and so is envy. For example, "Excuses offered to ward off acceptance of an emotional situation."

Knowing

Possessing knowledge, information, or understanding. A person showing cleverness, awareness

[16]Relationship Rocket science | A little bit about jealousy... relationshiprocketscience.com.au/a-little-bit-about-jealousy

and resourcefulness; A person described as shrewd. Suggestive of secret or private knowledge: *a knowing glance*. Deliberate; conscious. People also deliberately formulate and offer excuses and present the same as reason. For example, "My knowledge of you is that you will not take it seriously."

Labelling

Labeling is describing someone or something in a word or short phrase. For example, describing someone who has broken a law as a criminal. Providing excuse because a label is already given to the other person or the situation. For example, "you are not a team player is the reason I did not involve you"

Nuisance

One that is inconveniencing, annoying, or vexatious; a bother: Using this impression to provide an excuse for not doing that which one is supposed to do or doing that which one is not supposed to do. "For example, "I did not take you serious…."

Ongoing

Ongoing implies a movement that is continuous, a process or work-in-progress. Excuses are used as an on-going process such as 'this is the way things are done here", for example, 'corruption' has been associated with excuses as reasons.

Perception

Percept: the representation of what is perceived; basic component in the formation of a concept; a way of conceiving something; sensing: becoming aware of something via the senses. Excuse can emanate from perception and it is always difficult to disprove such excuses. For example, "This is the way I see it..."

Querying

In general, a query is a form of questioning, in a line of inquiry. Rather than admit the ignorance or non-acceptance of a situation, the excuser presents his/her views as though there was some form of ambiguity in the air. For example, "Did you really mean it?"

Rescuing

Rescue refers to operations that usually involve the saving of life, or prevention of injury. This as an excuse which is very often used to protect oneself and/or other significant persons in one's life/environment. For example, "He did it because...."

Symptoms

A symptom is a departure from normal function or feeling which is noticeable indicating the presence of abnormality. It can be a trait or body language that indicates when one is giving excuses. It can also be a mark of threat to the individual which causes him/her to present excuses as reasons. For example, "I read your body language as Threatening"

Taunting

A method in hand-to-hand combat, sarcastic remark, or insult intended to demoralize the recipient, or to anger and encourage reactionary behaviors without thinking. To reproach in a mocking, insulting, or contemptuous manner. For example, "Mocking an individual in pretence in such a way as if you were being honest."

Underrating

Underrating - an estimation that is too low; an estimate that is less than the true or actual value. Not wanting to connect or relate can be as a result of underrating the other person or the situation but several other excuses are provided as the reason for not engaging. For example, providing an excuse for "not accepting and invitation because you think that you are superior to the other person."

Vulnerability

A person who is susceptible to physical or emotional injury is always looking for a way to avoid situations that can cause harm or injury. Excuses are strong weapons to protect one's own vulnerability. For example, "fear of rejection can be a reason for not taking initiative towards relationship."

Wanting

Wanting to belong or to be controlled but not showing it directly. This need can be masked with several excuses. For example, claiming that one is at his/her best as a loner when the need is actually to belong.

Xerophyte

Excuses, like xerophyte survive in the midst of less acceptance, values, self-esteem and social status. For example, "when values clash and one does not want to accept or state the obvious."

Yearning

Craving to be truthful but dreading to be perceived as weak or powerless; hence, excuses take over yearning to be straightforward. For example, "the fear of rejection."

Zealot (resistance)

One who strongly believes in his understanding and does not even want to listen to others and their views about the belief.

It appears that less is known about the different strategies involved in this explanation of, or preparation for, failure According to Dr. C.R. Snyder,[17] clinical

---

[17]Synder, C.R., Higgings, R.L. & Stucy, R.J. (1983), Excuses: Masquerades in search of grace. John Wiley & Sons: New-York

psychologist at the University of Kansas, men and women make an equal number of excuses, but women use a verbally more sophisticated strategy, as opposed to men's macho bold-faced denial, or self- alibis for poor performance.

Starting back in early childhood, parents who love their children very much can still expect a great deal from them, and set standards accordingly. Years later, these same children often catch themselves making "excuses" for not living up to those standards. Dr. Snyder points out that self-concept develop in the early school years when children begin learning to compare their idealized version of themselves with reality. Seven-year-olds start worrying about what others think of them and by the age of nine kids start dealing with the concept of self-criticism.

Excuse making becomes a way of protecting young egos. Children sometimes feel that criticism is tantamount to epic rejection. After reading Dr. Snyder's theories, many of us can probably identify with techniques we use in our own excuse making process. Plain and simple "denial of responsibility" is one of the most common. For example, delay in submission of reports.

Why People Use Excuses[18]

The California State University Classroom Management Resource website[19] states in an article called "Excuse and Responsibility Psychology" that there are two primary reasons why people make excuses:

- Impression Management - The excuse-maker is attempting to look good in front of someone they want to impress, or there is a gap between their real and ideal selves.
- Situation Management - The excuse-maker believes an excuse might improve the outcome of some situation, salvage his/her self-image, or satisfy an authority figure.

An elaborate response to the reason for excuses include

- We use excuses to try to get out of personal responsibility because we are afraid of getting in trouble or the punishment it brings about.
- We use excuses to hide our faults and insecurities because they hide our incompetence.
- We use excuses to protect our own interest because truth hurts

---

[18]Lawrence, suite101 contributor since Aug 27, 2008.- Excuses and Excuse-Makers - COGNITIVE PSYCHOLOGY

[19]www.calstatela.edu/.../Excuse and Responsibility Psychol..

- We use excuses to justify ourselves to get out of trouble, to not feel bad about ourselves, and make it easy for others to move on etc.
- We 'feel' ashamed, for some dark and mysterious reason only known to us.
- We give excuses, because we are not capable of facing the reality that we are irresponsible on not doing a job.

We also give excuses to hide the real reason and not to hurt the other person especially our loved ones. In this case, excuses appear to be the only way to be sensitive to others feelings without being so inconsiderate with the situation.

People seldom do what they believe in. They do what is convenient, and then repent.[20] (Bob Dylan). But there's more to it than repentance, including: distraction, forgetting, trivialization, self-affirmation and denial of responsibility to name a few.[21]

Types of Excuses

Excuses are most often made to shift blame or boost self-image, but some people make excuses to pre-empt failure. Excuses are a common part of life, from the

---

[20]Bob Dylan - Witty Sayings
www.buzzle.com/articles/witty-sayings.html

[21]Understanding procrastination and how to achieve our goals by Timothy A. Pychy – Psychology Today, November 18, 2009

familiar "the dog ate my homework" to more complex psychological or emotional arguments over why something did or did not happen. Although people are motivated to make excuses, for a variety of reasons and under a multitude of circumstances, yet psychologists have begun to examine why some people become chronic "excuse-makers" as a way of coping with perceived inadequacies or fears. While the definition of the word "excuse" is somewhat slippery, an excuse is generally defined as a message transmitted from one person to another that either shifts blame for some situation or occurrence away from oneself or is made to help protect one's self-image. The purpose, is to move "...the source of negative feedback away from the protagonist."[22]

The discussion of excuses in Social Cognitive Psychology breaks excuses into two main categories.

Apparent-responsibility - The excuse-maker is striving to break the linkage to the negative outcome. "I didn't do it" is a common assertion of personal innocence that blames outside forces or cuts connection to group that has performed negatively. This type of excuse absolves one of personal responsibility by "cutting off reflected failure."

[22]Social Cognitive Psychology, 1997 David F. Barone, James E. Maddux, and C. R. Snyder

Transformed-responsibility - The excuse-maker admits to being linked to the negative outcome, but tries to steer clear of responsibility. A common phrase people use when engaging in this type of excuse is "Yes, but...," after which they elaborate on why they shouldn't be strongly associated with the negative outcome.[23]

People normally use excuses after a negative outcome presents itself. People also become adept at making excuses in anticipation of poor performance. For example, avoiding activities or situations where one might not do well is one way of anticipatory excuse-making;

Self-handicapping, where an individual introduces an impediment that supposedly hinders adequate performance, thus providing a ready-made place to transfer blame when things go wrong.

Research discussed in the January 5, 2009 New York Times article by Benedict Carey, "Some Protect the Ego By Working on Their Excuses Early"[24] reveals that men are more prone than women to self-handicapping, according to work done by Edward R. Hirt, a psychologist at Indiana University. In a study

---

[23]**Excuses and Excuse-Makers | Suite101** *suite101.com/article/excuses-and-excusemakers-a128935* Share

[24]Mind - Some Protect the Ego by Working on Their Excuses Early ... www.nytimes.com/2009/01/06/health/06mind.html

by Sean McCrea, a psychologist at the University of Konstanz, Germany who was cited in the same article, it was shown that given the opportunity and the right incentive, most people will claim a handicap when things don't go well, primarily because it helps them cushion the blow that failure can land to their self-confidence. McCrea goes on to say that handy excuses are also used as a way to rationalize that an individual did the best he could, and can cause a drop in motivation to improve performance on subsequent tasks by removing the potential for embarrassment.

Excuse and Reason

Two roads diverged in a wood, and I --I took the one less travelled by,

And that has made all the difference.
(Robert Frost, 1915)

I didn't know it was so urgent.
I was so much busy, couldn't find time for it.
I thought I had told you.
These things take time.
The customer was unreasonable.
It just slipped out of my mind.[25]

A reason is an explanation. An excuse makes it sound like it was okay.

When you make excuses you are essentially coming up with reasons that are based on some kind of dishonesty. Excuse is a justification for giving up or giving in. Excuses are reasons that rely upon your being dishonest with others and yourself.

---

[25]**Ezinearticles.com** - Excuse Or Reason - Does it Make Any Difference? By **Ashok Grover**

Reason lives you with no choice as there is just that one reason that prevented you from living up to expectation. A classic illustration of this is given in http://fishyvb.something-fishy.org/showthread. php?t=70449 "I was late because of a horrible accident on the highway. They closed the road and we were stuck with no way to get off for two hours. Reason! You didn't have a choice. You were surrounded by other cars equally stuck and had no choice but to wait until the traffic personnel could figure out how to get everyone safely detoured. No amount of pre-planning would have changed it."

The ability to make an excuse relies upon choice, while reason is not based on choice because in reason you are thoroughly handicapped as in the case of the traffic jam mentioned above. I was late because I overslept. Excuse! You had choices to figure out what time to wake up. Ask someone to wake you up, set your clock alarm, etc. You didn't plan ahead properly because for some reason it wasn't important to you to be on time. At the same time, you were not sensitive to those who were waiting for you or whom you promised to deliver something to, at a particular time.

How many times have you paid late fee while settling bills such as electricity or telephone bills, because you waited until the last minute. What would be your reason for not paying a bill that is due and that need be paid, all you have is excuse in this regard.

An excuse is what you use to justify doing or not doing something. A reason is accepting responsibility for it.[26] A reason is an explanation based on something, over which you had no control.

An excuse is an explanation used to exonerate oneself from irresponsibility. It is but natural to say that one has been giving excuses but the fact remains that the other person or party will come to know some day. I am not sure which is easier to bear, the immediate admission that you are giving an excuse or the later discover of the other person or party that you have been dishonest. But, I am sure, you have been aware of your own excuses, when and how to use them and for what justifications you employ. You need to ask yourself if there is an established pattern that has become apparent and if this practice has brought years of misery on yourself. Do you still want to continue with it? You know, you should look forward and not back, but you have these rather annoying rear-view mirrors which are hard to avoid...

Obviously, there will be genuine reasons for not completing an assignment and the regrets that follow it. However, in most cases, rather than share this feeling of shame of inability to live up to expectation or to deliver your promises, lots of time is spent on fabricating

[26] An Excuse vs. A Reason [Archive] - SFWED Remember It Hurts Community fishyvb.something-fishy.org/archive/index.php/t-70449.htmlShare05-05-2003

what would appear as a sound reason to the aggrieved party. This must have been in the mind of prolific English author and poet, Rudyard Kipling, when he said "We have forty million reasons for failure, but not a single excuse." While excuses are our masks for covering our shame of dishonesty, reasons tend to explain why we have failed. It is interesting to note that when things are not the way we would want it to be, we always find a scapegoat to lay the blame on.

Nothing happens because of me, it is because of one thing or the other. True, sometimes things are not under your control and you may have valid reasons; but, even in most of such cases, thorough and discrete investigation will reveal that it was because of your actions. Take the example of paying the bills procrastination.

Now, just think for a while, if the job you promised to someone is not done, does it really make any difference to him/her whether you have a valid reason or a stupid excuse for not doing it? It might (or might not) change his/her views or feelings about you; but will not change the end result. And, over a period of time, people understand how well or bad you are in giving excuses as reasons. You are then branded and in most cases it is difficult to disassociate you from excuses even when you give genuine and valid reasons.

Just think about yourself and your environment. Are there people that you have branded as excuse-makers whenever they attempt to tell you why they did not do what they are supposed to do? Are there people whose statements you brand inariably as excuses, even before they try to explain to you?

Reasons explain why things are as they are, meaning that you are accepting the accountability for the same. Excuses also explain why things are as they are; but puts blame on, or shifts accountability to, someone else, who is not there to explain or defend—be it a person or situational circumstances. Have you noticed that the person, to whom an excuse is given as reason, has no one present to verify the authenticity of such information?

Another distinction is that reasons come much earlier than the deadline and move a person to take corrective action, which in most of the cases are immediate, or at least for future. Excuses come after the deadlines have passed and reappear again and again. While reasons force you to make amends and keep you charged, excuses bring in a sense of helplessness.[27]

Check this out yourself. Consider those situations where you have given excuses as reason and the situations have given genuine reason for a job not done, a promise not fulfilled, a commitment not honoured. Did you notice that you give excuse for those activities

---

[27]safiya hoskins | Beauty, Brains & the Bottom Line beautybrainsandthebottomline.wordpress.com/tag/safiya-hoskins/

which are within our control and which can find a way or the other to do, but you fail to do them. Notice also that all the places you have given genuine reasons are situations where you could not have done anything irrespective of your desperation to keep your promise.

Interestingly, the other party understands no matter how smart you may think you are. It may not come back to you; but it is so much habit forming. Forget about 'bad' and 'good' excuses. All excuses are bad, because giving up accountability always leads to moving yourself into negative spiral of personal growth. An excuse is a reason justified by dishonesty. It is not only being dishonest to others; but to yourself as well. Have you noticed that excuses give you a momentary relief and if discovered can give you a perpetual pain.

In the words of HV Adolt, "We are all manufacturers. Making good, making trouble, or making excuses."[28] Choice is ours. Do remember what Benjamin Franklin said, "He that is good for making excuses is seldom good for anything else." Obviously it isn't black and white. There are "excuses" that do little harm to anyone. There are reasons that produce great harm. But it's important to recognize how you might be making excuses and trying to justify them as a valid reason.

---

[28]quotationsbook.com/quote/5059/

It is but conventional for people to offer excuses that also serve as reason. The major culprit for such excuses being "Time". How many times have you used lack of time as an excuse for not doing what you are supposed to do? When you offer such responses as "I don't know what to do or what to say", do you offer it as an excuse or reason? Who would ask you to do or say something that you have no idea about?

There are examples that would serve both as excuse or reason. For example, in many instances in my practice, I have heard such comments as "my father is aggressive and says he was raised by an aggressive father and, as a result, he is also aggressive. Does this excuse his behaviour or could he have found another way? You may have reason for what you do but the reason might not excuse your action - murder, rape, non-cooperation, physical attack, accepting bribes are examples.

In more common instances of having no time to write, invest in relationship, exercise, undertake minor repairs or cleaning in the house or working in the garden, does it really mean that there is no time or that you have not made up your mind to do what is needed to be done? What is the honest answer here, did you not have the time or was it simply not a priority?

When people are confronted about the state of relationships with each other, there are always responses which indicate that the relationship is taken for granted by assuming that there is nothing wrong in the relationship, yet the question arises? Rather than this type of evasive response, it will serve to have a frank conversation with this person about how you are feeling. Talk about the problem, then, if you feel it is best to step away from the friendship, be honest about that and tell the other person.

In practice, rather than talking to the person, you talk about the person. When you talk to a person, you are looking at that person's face and talking but when you talk about a person, observe that the person is, in most cases, not available in the same place where you are talking about him. I have noticed this pressure of having to pretend that all is well with a 'so-called' friend when nothing is well at all. One thing that I laud myself for, in recent times, is my ability to state it up front and let the other person know how I feel about it. I have noticed that this attitude strengthens rather than threatens our relationship.

It is important in any relationship to realize that people make mistakes or fails to live up to the expectation. I see that what is more irritating, more annoying, more frustrating is really not what is not done but the excuse presented as reason for not doing that.

How do you feel about a customer who offers excuses every time the customer falls short of expectations? It is obvious that the feeling is not a good one and if this continues, it is likely that you will take the easiest route to get away from such unreliable client. Using an excuse only makes you seem untrustworthy, instead of making your actions seem justifiable. A simple 'I am sorry, I will see that the problem is fixed' is always better than a litany of excuses or multiple apologies. This could explain why some of the BPOs close as soon as they open because their inability to meet deadlines is explained with flimsy excuses that the client is aware of. The result is loss of trust and confidence in the ability to provide the work as and when required.

It is a natural impulse to want to be forgiven or pardoned when you make a mistake. Remember that whoever is dealing with the said problem does not have the time to also make you feel better as well. Sometimes, it is hard to realize when an excuse is leaving your lips. How can you tell if a reason is really just an excuse? A good rule is that if you had ample opportunity to change the result and you didn't, then it's an excuse.

All is not lost, however; people are most impressive when they are able to calmly fix a difficult situation. So think of each mistake as a moment to inspire confidence.

❑❑❑

Part-II

Intrapersonal Effects of Excuses

Intrapersonal Effects

Intrapersonal is the internal being that runs within an individual and which defines and reveals the type of relationship one has with one self. It is a reflection of who one is and is governed by one's ability to look into oneself and admit what is seen. This means that attention is to be given to the choice of language, the meaning making process, and understanding of self motivation. Taking accountability for understanding your motivations, interpretations and personal biases lends insight into how our perspectives and perceptions affect our interactions with the world outside of us. How would you define yourself? Intrapersonal awareness is a prelude to owning one's flaws, it is the personal accountability that results when time and effort are spent to understand and design a competency model for internal dialogue and external expression. Building a strong relationship with the self is the aspiration of many who go out of the way to search for peace and tranquillity. Intrapersonal communication occurs within our intimate world. We have to take charge of that world and make it congruent upon our needs, a reality that supports nourishing and nurturing our emotional wellbeing. But this congruence gets disturbed when we fail to say the truth, or when we say everything except the truth.

Emotional intelligence requires us to be constantly aware of our 'here and now', not to drift, as that is the only way we can invariably get in touch with our existential reality. It is a struggle to admit and express vulnerability, as a result of our assumptions about others or about ourselves. When we give excuses, this equilibrium is disturbed and it is difficult, cumbersome and time-consuming to come back to that level. It means that the search and the struggle for existence continue.

Goal achievement is a good measure of intrapersonal equilibrium and is a strong self motivating factor. Nothing succeeds like success is a saying that we all know. When one sets a goal and achieves it, he/she takes complete ownership even when there are others that contributed to this; those people are mentioned in passing, if at all they are mentioned. On the other hand, when the goal is not achieved, there is denial of responsibility and the blame goes to some other person except the individual who failed to achieve the goal. Excuse becomes the nearest and the best weapon to exonerate one self from one's failure to deliver, rather than becoming vulnerable for a sustainable change.

❑❑❑

Excuses and Dissonance

The only man who is really free is the one who can turn down an invitation to dinner without giving an excuse

—Jules

Cognitive dissonance is a discomfort caused by holding conflicting cognitions, for example, ideas, beliefs, values, emotions) simultaneously. People in a state of dissonance, may feel surprise, dread, guilt, anger, or embarrassment. The theory of cognitive dissonance in social psychology proposes that people have a motivational drive to reduce dissonance by altering existing cognitions or adding new ones to create consistency.[29]

Leon Festinger in his 1956 book "When Prophecy Fails" chronicled the followers of a UFO cult as reality clashed with their fervent belief in an impending apocalypse. Cognitive dissonance is one of the most influential and extensively studied theories in social

[29]cognitive disequilibrium | hydrogen2oxygen www.hydrogen2oxygen.net/en/tag/cognitive-disequilibrium/

psychology. **Cognitive disequilibrium**[30] is a closely related concept in the cognitive developmental theory of Jean Piaget: the inevitable conflicts a child experiences between current beliefs and new information, will lead to disequilibrium, which, in turn, motivates the child's progress through the various stages of development.

Cognitive dissonance theory warns that people have a bias to seek consonance among their cognitions. This bias gives the theory its predictive power, shedding light on otherwise puzzling irrational and even destructive behavior.

A classical illustration of cognitive dissonance is expressed in the fable *The Fox and the Grapes by Aesop.*[31] In the story, a fox sees some high-hanging grapes and wishes to eat them. When the fox is unable to think of a way to reach them, he decides that the grapes are probably not worth eating, with the justification the grapes probably are not ripe or that they are sour (hence "sour grapes"). This example follows a pattern: one desires something, finds it unattainable, and reduces one's dissonance by criticizing it. Jon Elster calls this pattern "adaptive preference formation".[32]

---

[31] **A Record of the Defense of The Gnostic Movement and Belzebuub** ... *gnosticfreedom.com* › Witness Accounts

[32] Elster, Jon. Sour Grapes: Studies in the Subversion of Rationality. Cambridge 1983, p. 123ff.

Probably, the most famous case in the early study of cognitive dissonance was described by Leon Festinger and others in the book *When Prophecy Fails*.[5] The authors infiltrated a religious group that was expecting the imminent end of the world on a certain date. When that date passed without the world ending, the movement did not disband. Instead, the group came to believe that they had been spared, in order to spread their teachings to others, a justification that resolved the conflict between their previous expectations and reality.

It is often easier to make excuses or pass judgment than it is to change behaviour or values; cognitive dissonance research contributes to the abundance of evidence in social psychology that humans are not always rational beings (Excuse Makers).

Since the 1950's with Leon Festinger's[33] (and his students') initial work on cognitive dissonance, psychologists have spent countless number of hours studying how acting counter-attitudinally leads to a negative emotional state. People want to live and maintain a positive sense of self by acting competently, morally, and to be able to predict their own behaviour. When our actions and beliefs, or even two beliefs, are in conflict, they are dissonant. Dissonance is uncomfortable. We want to relieve ourselves from this

[33]Cognitive Dissonance Theory of Leon Festinger - By: Amy Schick

negative state. Any form of excuse which constitutes a "lie" eases this mental conflict, despite the fact that efforts are made to hide this from people.

This relief is seen in the form of attitudinal change with the belief that if my behaviour conflicts with my own attitude, then I need to change my attitude altogether. Change in attitude here is taken for granted and can be easily changed; as such, it is the road most journeyed. However, even Festinger has argued that this isn't simple or easy (and it's seldom the preferred route; it's the road less journeyed). As Dylan has noted, it's easier to do what's convenient, not necessarily what we believe in, than repent.

Not only do "people seldom do what they believe in" but all too often people don't do what they intend to do. They do what is convenient (what they feel like). There is a wide gap between what people know and what they do. When we intend to act, when we have a goal to which we've made an intention to act, and we don't act (voluntarily and quite irrationally, choosing to delay action, in spite of knowing this may affect us negatively), we experience dissonance. This is one of the costs of procrastination which is commonly experienced emotionally as guilt, and people engage in alternative strategies more often, with the avowed objective of reducing the dissonance; or do whatever they can in order to get rid of this negative emotion created by procrastination. Here are a few typical reactions that researchers have catalogued as responses to dissonance (and ways that people choose to reduce its negative impact).

1. **Distraction :** allows individuals to divert their attention away from their dissonant cognitions and avoid the negative effect of the state caused by dissonance;
2. **Forgetting :** can be in two forms, passive and active. Passive is often the case with inconsequential thoughts, while we may have to actively suppress important cognitions that are causing dissonance;
3. **Trivialization :** involves changing beliefs to reduce the importance of the dissonance creating thoughts or beliefs;
4. **Self-affirmation :** creates a focus on our core values and other qualities that reasserts our sense of self and integrity, despite the dissonance;
5. **Denial of Responsibility :** allows us to distance ourselves as a causal agent in the dissonance;
6. **Adding Consonant Cognitions :** often by seeking out new information that supports our position; and
7. **Changing Behaviour :** to better align with our beliefs and values, although changing one's behaviour requires effort and is often not the most convenient way to reduce dissonance.[34]

[34]Procrastination, Guilt, Excuses and the Road Less Traveled ... www.psychologytoday.com/.../procrastination-guilt-excuses-and-the-roa

There are many strategies available at our disposal to make people feel good as they minimize feelings of dissonance, and people have perfected the deployment of these strategies in order to keep buoyant day-to-day. It's part of the coping mechanisms, but all coping mechanisms are not adaptive. Quite consistently, research has demonstrated that techniques like distraction, forgetting, trivialization and denial of responsibility are emotion-charged strategies that are not nearly as effective in the long run as planned-problem-solving strategies.

Understandably, we have to take care of our emotions, but this can't be where the coping stops. If it were, that would just be a case of "giving in to feel good," and we'll pay in the long run if this is our dominant short-term strategy.

What we're doing actually is making excuses for ourselves to bolster a threatened sense of self. Why is self threatened? In the case of procrastination, it's because we failed to self-regulate and do an intended task in a timely manner. Interestingly, we're the only one to blame as we become our own worst enemy. The sad answer seems to be to entrench a little deeper into self-protection. I think it is high time that we lived with the tension that cognitive dissonance creates, and let it fuel more honesty; perhaps, an honest look at behavioural changes.

❑❑❑

Excuses and Emotions

And oftentimes excusing of a faulty
Doth make the fault the worse by the excuse

—William Shakespeare

Making excuses is a common phenomenon all over the world. Human beings are social animals who do not live in isolation but depend upon other's care, love, concern, and affection, with a sense of belongingness and inclusion. There is nobody who does not want to experience acceptance and belongingness. It is precisely for this reason that the opinions and actions of other people matter a lot to an individual. The emotional interest people have shown in others is all pervasive. On many occasions, our actions are questioned or criticized by others, or even by ourselves. Sometimes we are required to explain and defend our actions, especially when the action does not have the desired effect or the action is least expected from the individual. It is the impact of this undesirable outcome or the meanness of the action that causes the receiving party to ask for explanation and the giving party has the tendency to say things that will justify its action, mainly through excuses.

Interestingly, it is the listener who attaches the label "excuse" to a statement made to him and the person who made the statement, though is aware that he/she is making an excuse, pretends as though he was giving a reason. But how does a person view a message or information passed on to him/her as an "excuse"? It stems from the emotional impact of the action or information, rather than the intuition of the receiver to judge a statement or information as an excuse.

There is an emotional connect that gets triggered when a message or information is received. There is an impact that raises doubt or belief in the mind of the receiver. If the impact is of doubtful characteristic, it means that the message or information has the tendency to cause harm to the receiver or sounds completely out of place in the convention of things. The receiver demands an explanation to enable him/her deal with this emotional impact.

On the side of the person passing on the information or message, we observe that not in all cases may the person feel uneasy because of questionable actions. If the context is such that we do not care about the person who views our actions as questionable, we will be indifferent as to what has happened, or is going to happen. For us to feel uneasy with our behaviour, not only must it be dubious, but also the one who questions it must be of some relevance to us.[35]

It means that if a behaviour or action is questioned, someone has the responsibility to provide an explanation and the need for explanation is that the behaviour or action has caused or has the tendency to cause uneasiness to the other person who demands explanation.

It is emotional bondage that triggers the need for explanation and again, it is emotional bondage that determines the choice of response that one makes in this circumstance.

(a) Avoidance : We avoid dealing with our responsibility or the outcomes of our actions either because we do not care about the situation, or do not feel obliged to invest any effort in changing its consequences; or because of our inability to improve our image by explaining the questionable action. In either case, it means that we are not ready to assume responsibility since the price may be considerably high; accordingly, we leave things as they are, hoping that the demand for an explanation will not be sustained with efflux of time, and the uneasiness associated with it will subside.

---

[35]Excuses, emotions and in between - the viewpoint of the listener Shlomo Hareli - Department of Psychology - University of Haifa
* Presented as a poster at the ISRE (International Society for Research on Emotions) Toronto, 1996

(b) Admission : We admit our responsibility and may also wish to be pardoned or forgiven. While here we are still being held responsible for the situation, we may restore our former positive image by being viewed as honest because of our admission and by that also relieve the uneasiness. Admission indicates that we are assuming the responsibility for our behaviour and are willing to face the consequences. In personal relationship, admission tends to build more bonding than denial or defence. However, in many cases, people think that by admission, the other party will likely walk away from the relationship. Just consider if you have come across a situation where the truth is revealed to you, how you felt about it and, on the contrary, how you felt when a lie is uttered to you.

(c) Defence : We try to eliminate or reduce the negative aspects associated with our action by offering some sort of explanation that will clear us from the blame for the dubious action. Typical types of defence are denial, justification and excuse. Questionable actions need to be defended when we are considered to be responsible for an undesirable or odd outcome. Offering such a defence should then refer to (*a*) our responsibility, and (*b*) the undesirable or odd nature of the outcome. When we are held responsible for an undesirable situation, we are to explain the reasons for our actions, in order that it may bring about an evaluation of the situation or the outcome, whereby it no longer may seem so negative.

Three types of explanation may be discerned:

Denial is where we deny and do not hold ourselves responsible for the undesirable, or odd outcome, but try to find a scapegoat to be held responsible.

Justification is an explanation which is aimed at eliminating or lessening the negative value of the outcome of a dubious action.

Excuse is an explanation which is aimed at eliminating or diluting our responsibility for a questionable action.

From either of the types of explanations cited above, observe that there is an agent who demands an explanation and another agent who supplies the explanation. Something is termed "denial", "justification" or "excuse" from the viewpoint of the listener—the agent supplying the information may consider it differently. The agent may be lying but as long as the listener is unable to detect the lie, though he /she may intuit something is "fishy", the explanation given will be considered as a justification or an excuse, rather than a lie. If we accept as justification the account rendered by another person, then, by definition, we cannot consider it as a lie. The same holds good for an explanation accepted as an excuse; if we know a person to be fully responsible for a certain outcome, we will not accept his or her explanation as an excuse but as a sheer lie.

There are two conditions that must be satisfied from the viewpoint of the listener, so that the explanation will be regarded as an excuse:[36]

The explanation leaves the situation indeterminate, *i.e.*, the explanation fails to establish that a better alternative to the dubious action was available. Accordingly, an excuse does little to relieve the emotional tension that has been created. The listener may still feel angry or even more disappointed after he/she has received the explanation.

The listener is unable to determine that the explanation holds no water. The explanation underlying an excuse may not be regarded as a lie from a corresponding criterion of truth, i.e., there are no known facts that clearly contradict it. But it would seem to be false from a coherent criterion of truth, that is, it is not consistent with our overall experience, attitudes, or beliefs. This characterization helps us explain the bad connotation associated with excuses.

Some writers are of the considered view an that excuse invariably is a type of lie. While an excuse is similar to a lie in the sense that it is being believed to involve false information, there is a substantive difference in the feeling it leaves with the listener.

---

[36]Austin, J. L. (1956a/1979), 'A Plea for Excuses',

Because of the wider criterion upon which such a belief is now based, there will never be complete certainty that the information provided is false.

In relating "emotions" and "excuses", it is to be understood that there are other factors that come into play in this game of excuses, as perceived by the listener. This discrepancy between the two—the excuse maker and the listener—emanates from some sort of relatedness.

In his Poster Presentation at the ISRE (International Society for Research on Emotions) Toronto, 1996, Shlomo Hareli - Department of Psychology - University of Haifa (Israel) grouped this relatedness into the following categories:

Knowledge of Reality : There are cases where the two parties possess different knowledge of facts related to the specific action. So, what may look as a good reason on the part of the excuse maker may look insufficient and unsatisfactory on the part of the listener who holds fewer, more, or different facts about the situation?

Attitudes : The two parties may differ in the importance and value they attach to the situation or to their relationship. So, what may be satisfying and adequate for the excuse maker, may be insufficient and improper for the listener.

Inflated Responsibility and Importance : Some social roles and positions, as well as people that hold them, may sometimes be perceived as involving more power and authority than they could actually contain. This may lead people to attach inflated responsibility to the one in such a position, and to feel that some issues are being dealt with in a less serious way than they ought to be. Therefore, any explanation on the part of someone holding such a position meant to reduce or eliminate responsibility or to treat the issue as trivial or severe will be seen as an excuse.

What is being emphasised in this chapter is that questionable actions, specifically when they involve damage, may cause negative emotions in those being hurt, and, in some cases, also in those that caused the damage.

Excuses are explanations aimed to repair one's self image, the emotional damage related to the loss of that self-image and the emotional damage caused to another agent, while trying to protect the listener from being emotionally hurt.[37]

Excuses typically do little by way of repairing the emotional damage caused, but usually succeed well where restoring one's self image is concerned and the emotional uneasiness associated with it.

---

[37]Weiner, B., Figueroa-Munoz, A., & Kakihara, C. (1991). The goals of excuses and communications strategies related to causal perceptions. Personality and Social Psychology Bulletin 17, 4-13.

Excuse, under some circumstances, can cause further exacerbation of the emotional tension between the parties involved, or even be the factor that will cause such a tension to arise. This is because of two main factors:

(i) as an unsatisfactory explanation, it may be perceived as continuing or even initiating the same sort of undesirable behaviour evolved by the questionable action, namely, hurting the listener; and

(ii) when the excuse is not accepted by the other side, the excuse maker may view this as a violation of the relationship and trust, especially, when from his/her point of view, the excuse given contains a satisfactory explanation.

❑❑❑

Excuses and Goal Achievement

"If you really want to do something, you'll find a way; If you don't, you'll find an excuse"

—Peter Shepherd

A goal is the desired result envisaged by a person or an organisation and which the individual plans and commits to achieve within a given time. It is the purpose or aim, the anticipated result or outcome of activity that will come in the form of physical or abstract object with intrinsic value.

Goal-setting involves setting specific, measurable, attainable, realistic and time-bounded (S.M.A.R.T.) objectives. There is no doubt that goal-setting can serve as an effective tool for making progress by ensuring that the individual or organisation has a clear awareness of what it must do to achieve an objective. On a personal level, the process of setting goals allows people to specify and then work towards their own objectives; most commonly, financial or career-based goals. Goal-setting comprises a major component of personal development.

A goal can be long-term or short-term. The primary difference is the time required to achieve them. Individuals can set personal goals, families can set family goals, organisations can set organisational goals. The fact is that goals provide direction of focus of the individual or the organisation. Knowing precisely what one wants to achieve makes it targeted and clear, as to what to concentrate and improve on; and often subconsciously prioritizes on such goals. Goal-setting and planning promotes long-term vision and short-term motivation. It focuses intention, desire, acquisition of knowledge, and helps to raise resources.

Efficient goal-setting includes recognizing and resolving all guilt, inner conflict or limiting belief that might cause one to sabotage one's efforts. By setting clearly defined goals, one can subsequently measure and take pride in the achievement of those goals. One can see progress in what might have seemed a long, perhaps impossible, grind. Achieving complex and difficult goals requires focus, long-term diligence and effort. Success in any field requires forgoing excuses and justifications for poor performance or lack of adequate planning; in short, success requires emotional maturity. Long-term achievements rely upon a series of short-term achievements.

There are two ways to live in this world. One is to live as though everything was a miracle and the other to live as if nothing was a miracle. Most people think success comes from good luck or enormous talent, but many successful people achieve their accomplishments in a simpler way: through a self-disciplined approach to their goals. Setting a goal is easy. Sticking to your commitment to reach that goal is where the real challenge lies.

I don't know about you, but I definitely have had my fair share of reasons for not accomplishing something I set out to do. Although I have seen myself making resolutions after resolutions, setting out goals using the so called "SMART" principle, defining and redefining priorities, yet fail to achieve the set goals when the time comes. There are some legitimate reasons why you might not complete a specific goal but there also are excuses. It is said that you either have result or you have excuses. . I have come to accept the saying that "The only thing standing between you and your goal is your lame excuse that you keep on telling yourself why you can't achieve it" An interesting observation I have made is that whenever I set out these goals which I have considered achievable, then I notice this gamut of excuses flowing from nowhere which puts across reasons why I should not be able to do it or why it would not succeed.

Procrastination is the first symptom of avoiding pursuit of goal or the first sign of indiscipline when it comes to pursuing goals, no matter how 'smart' the goal has been set. The immediate choice is that this cannot be done now, then follows the excuses such as lack of time and/other resources. But these are actually nothing when one is focused and is passionate about the goal. Walt Disney was bankrupt and a small-time advertising man until he thought about Mickey Mouse and we all know the history today.

A goal is not something that is achieved out of convenience or ease. It is something that at first might seem unattainable. It requires planning, discipline and consistency to follow through. We all have to be real with ourselves, examine our priorities and make a commitment to follow through. I am busy. Life itself is busy, everybody is busy and we all have things we need to do. At the end of the day, it boils down to priorities. If it's important to you, you'll find the time to do it. I like to tell myself there's no reason why I can't. While we set goals that makes us to look up and climb the ascending steps, in implementation, our steps are made of 'excuses' that make it easy to descend on the steps and obviously go opposite the set goal.

What is unique about excuses is that it presents itself as good reasons for not taking the requisite steps and somewhere we are aware of it and seem to collude to sabotage ourselves. The fact is that these seemingly good reasons are not validated and we do not even think of doubting them for verification. Just think about it yourself. How many times have you stopped doing something, because somewhere you thought it will not work as planned? How many times have you stopped yourself from taking initiative to pursue your goal because you find reason not to do so? Is it really reason or is it an excuse? My experience has been that when I push something forward and say today or this time is not ripe for the activity, I feel good that I am able to think about the next right time. I have seen that when the next right time comes, the same excuses that I used to push the action till now surfaces with stronger explanations why waiting is necessary. Today I am guided by the dictum that "The best time to plant a tree was 20 years ago and the next best time is "Now."

The impact of excuses on goal achievement is not only at the individual level but also at the professional as well as the organisational level. Excuses for not achieving goals vary from individual to individual and from organisation to organisation and there is no one-size fits in all kinds of approach, to ensure that excuses do not derail goal achievement. Moreover, it is difficult for organisations to understand and deal with that sort of excuses emerging from

- low Goal Efficacy (when the individual has a low belief in his/her ability to achieve the desired goal, this is explained by what the individual presents as reason, rather than admitting that he/she is making excuses.

- low Goal Integrity (how consistent one's goal is with the core aspects of the individual), this is very common in organisations.

A model that looks at the sequence of steps that need be followed from the commencement to the attainment of goal (Self-concordance model)[38] looks at the impact of goal achievement on an individual. It is assumed that the impact depends on the type of goal and meaning of the goal to the individual. The model distinguishes factors that promote striving to achieve a goal, achieving a goal and the factors that connect goal achievement to changes in subject well-being.

Self-concordant goals fulfill basic needs and aligns with an individual's True Self and these goals have personal meaning to the individual and reflect an individual's self-identity, self-concordant goals are more likely to receive sustained effort overtime. On the other hand, goals that do not reflect the individual's internal drive and are pursued due to external factors emerge from a non-integrated region of a person and are, therefore, more likely to be abandoned when obstacles occur.[39]

---

[38]Sheldon, Kennon M.; Eliott, Andrew J. (1999). "Goal Striving, Need Satisfaction and Longitudinal Well-Being: The Self-Concordance Model.". Journal of Personality and Social Psychology 76 (3): 482-497.

[39]Gollwitzer, P.M. (1990). E.T Higgins &R.M. Sorrentino, ed. Handbook of motivation and cognition(2 ed.). New York: Guilford Press. pp. 53-92.

Organizationally, goal management consists of the process of recognizing or inferring goals of individual team-members, abandoning no longer relevant goals, identifying and resolving conflicts among goals, and prioritizing goals consistently for optimal team-collaboration and effective operations.

An organizational goal-management solution ensures that individual employee goals and objectives align with the vision and strategic goals of the entire organization. Goal-management provides organizations with a mechanism to effectively communicate corporate goals and strategic objectives to each person across the entire organization. The key consists of having it all emanate from a pivotal source and providing each person with a clear, consistent organizational-goal message. With goal-management, every employee understands how their efforts contribute to an enterprise's success.

We are mostly nervous about new things in our lives. If you're hesitant with the goal you have to achieve then it will never fail you to seek advice from professional who is dealing with the goal you are to attain. Once you understand what you have to do accept the reality that anxiety may come but proceed with your goal anyway.

But look at excuses such as

"I don't want to fail so........"

"It isn't my fault......"

"Life get's in the way"

"I tried but something came up..."

"I am not good enough or the right person...."

"I am too old or too young....."

And other such statements, do they sound as reasons or excuses and does any of them motivate you to even give your goal a try. However, when you were formulating the goal in your mind, you understood that this is what you deserve and that is what you want. But during the implementation phase, several reasons why you should not pursue your goal emerge and none of them tells you why you do not deserve the outcome.

❑❑❑

Excuses and Lies

"I'm not upset that you lied to me, I'm upset that from now on I can't believe you"

—Friedrich Nietzsche

I am sure that many people reading this book sometimes make excuses or tell lies as reason. How can one distinguish between a lie and an excuse?

A lie is an untrue statement from one person or group to another person or group who knows the truth but intentionally refuses to say the truth to the other person or group. An excuse is a reason for something to happen or not to happen. An excuse is not always a lie but a lie is always a lie which is hundred per cent untrue. Excuse is a reason given for action/inaction that could be true or false whereas lie is untruth, said to cover up. An excuse is an attempt to justify a certain behaviour or action. A lie is an untruth meant to deceive, the reasons for which could be many.

"To excuse" means to grant or obtain an exemption. A lie is an untruthful statement made to someone else with the intention to deceive. To lie is to say something one believes to be false with the intention that it be taken for the truth by someone else.

Once a lie is told, the liar has this tendency to sound victorious because, the other person has been deceived without his/her knowledge and the liar has had his/her way. In my experience, this has proved as wrong an assumption on the part of the liar. When my son was 11 years old, and while in a discussion, he stated that, "if you tell one lie, you will need another 25 lies to cover it up." It means that lies need to be protected otherwise it will be discovered; but when the liar is telling the lie, he/she puts the lie with such deceitful confidence as though it cannot be discovered. The fact is that lots of energy will be required to protect the lie from being discovered but how long can one consciously protect a lie? As Mark Twain rightly put it "One of the most striking differences between a cat and a lie is that a cat has only nine lives" while an African proverb has it that 'all the days are for the robber, but one day is for the owner of the house being robbed." Let us, therefore, look at the consequences of lies rather than looking at the illusion of lies not being identified.

Consequences of Lies

A lie is an untruthful statement whose intention is always to mislead or deceive. The saying that "you cannot have a liar without a lie," indicates that lie is a conscious effort to mislead. Telling lies is, therefore, a choice between the "truth" and "lie." The person telling lies knows that he/she is not telling the truth but tells lies which he/she considers inconsequential or feeble, especially when not much is at stake. However, each bit of lie no matter how subtle has consequences for the liar.

Cognitive Dissonance

As noted in an earlier chapter, cognitive dissonance is the discomfort that one feels when one holds two contradicting ideas or two conflicting thoughts in mind, in this case, to tell the truth or to lie. This state of mind is aggravated when one tells a lie. You can check this out yourself as to how your heartbeats respond when you tell a lie. Many times, lies are told to appease the other person such as saying that something is good when it is really not good or that something is unimportant when it is really important. Have you not reported that all is well when you are really irritated with someone?

The fact is that such lies are considered harmless; hence, ignored as they rarely resurface in future conversation. However, their existence and practice can become a habit that would have long term effects even as their consequences seem benign or even non-existent in the short run.

Lies affect Health

And you shall know the truth, and the truth shall make you free (The Bible).[40] What is truth? Truth is the story or narration of what really happened and nothing more or less. In telling the truth, all you need to do is to remember what happened and state it verbatim and your job is over.

On the other hand, lying requires several considerations:

i. What is to be hidden from the other person

ii. Construct a believable opposite of what really happened.

iii. Formulate the words and strategy to present it to the other person in a form that is convincing.

iv. Remember it for a very long time if not for a life time to ensure that you are never caught.

The pressure adds up and builds even if you do not know it, every time you tell lies. Unfortunately, mankind is guilty of lies. According to Pamela Meyer, "The average person lies three times within the first minute of meeting a stranger and between 10 and 200 times per day. We handle this constant lying well considering how remarkably often it occurs, but that's especially easy to do when we have an easy time ignoring the consequences."[41]

---

[40]The Bible: John 18:32

[41]http://www.ted.com/speakers/pamela_meyer.html

All of us experience stress in our everyday life. No one escapes stress especially as we need some level of stress to be motivated. But we are all like the rubber band which can be stretched not to any maximum but to its own maximum. Some will stretch longer because of their thickness and some will just stretch and break. This indicates that each rubber band has it's level of elasticity and beyond this level, the band will cut. This is true with human beings as each possess its own degree of elasticity or resilience. It is not a one size fit all type of elasticity, hence, one should understand what stretches one beyond one's elasticity level.

We need energy to do whatever we want or asked to do. Part of this energy is sometimes directed to some other activities that do not contribute to the activity in hand. One such direction is using part of the available energy to protect lies and forcing ourselves to use the remaining energy to achieve what really matters. The fact that the required energy is less after having been divided reduces our ability and motivation to push forward. Frustration, anger, bitterness...step in but we readily point to our outside as the cause for our unhappiness. Whatever happens, you know the truth. You even tell lies to yourself. Own up that you are protecting something and be free from stress.

When I ask my participants to make a list of their stressors, I invite them to write down all that make them gnash their teeth, tighten their faces, all that cause the rate of their heart beat to increase, irritates and so on, no matter how trivial. Many people come up with traffic jam, things are not where they are supposed to be, children not taking their studies seriously, cell phone menace among youth and several other things. When they are asked to make a list of all of these stressors that are in their hand or which they can manage, the result is astounding and the relief is worth the exercise.

I rarely have come across anybody reporting that his telling lies is a concern for him/her though there are several issues of people getting stressed because someone - spouse, child, subordinate, boss - tells lots of lies. But who does not tell lies? I think it is the denial that one tells lies or not admitting to oneself that one has told a lie that causes stress. In other words, stress caused by telling lies can be controlled by admitting that one has told lies or by saying the truth.

While there is extensive literature on 'Lies', but suffice it here to say the following:-[42]

- An excuse has been defined as the skin of reason stuffed with a lie.
- An excuse is a reason for something to happen or not happen. An excuse isn't always a lie. A lie, is something that is 100% not true.
- A lie is intentional. An excuse is unavoidable .

[42]http://qna.rediff.com/questions-and-answers/whats-the-difference-between-an-excuse-a-lie/16336585/answers

- Excuse is a reason given for your inaction/action that could be true or false whereas lie is untruth, said to cover up.
- An excuse is worse and more terrible than a lie; because an excuse is a cover for a lie.
- Excuse could be genuine or non-genuine.

  Lie is obviously non-genuine.

Part-III

Interpersonal Effects of Excuses

Interpersonal Effects

Interpersonal implies dealing with others rather than dealing with self. In order to be and work with others, there has to be some connection that links one person to the other in relationship. Interpersonal relationships exist between any two or more persons who interact and fulfill one or more physical or emotional needs of the other. The closest relationships are most often found with family and a small circle of the best friends. Interpersonal relationships require the most effort to nurture and maintain.

Interpersonal skills are the life skills we use every day to communicate and interact with other people, both individually and in groups. People who have worked on developing strong interpersonal skills are usually more successful in both their professional and personal lives.

Interpersonal skills are so important that employers often seek to hire staff with **'strong interpersonal skills'** - they want people who will work well in a team and be able to communicate effectively with colleagues, customers and clients.

Interpersonal skills are not just important in the workplace, our personal and social lives can also benefit from better interpersonal skills. People with good interpersonal skills are usually perceived as optimistic, calm, confident and charismatic qualities that are often endearing or appealing to others.

The strength of this relationship between two or more people for any common purpose is affected by

- what is said and how it is said
- body language
- listening and interpreting
- working with others to find solutions
- working with others to identify, define and solve problems
- decision making process
- freedom to communicate values, ideas, beliefs needs and wants

These are also the relationships that give you the most joy and satisfaction. An interpersonal relationship is an association between two or more people that may range from fleeting to enduring. According to a 2010 article in Time magazine, challenges in life may feel less daunting to people with close interpersonal relationships. The magazine notes that close emotional connections and relationships may provide a sense of safety and security that reduces stress and promotes good health.

In this section, we take a look at how excuses can affect interpersonal relationships, personal effectiveness and decision making - personal or professional.

Excuses and Relationships

It is wise to direct your anger towards problems - not people, to focus your energies on answers - not excuses

—William Arthur Ward

In the short-term, excuses are merely an exercise in self-delusion, but over a period of time, those who engage in repeated excuses damage relationships. People view the tendency to make excuse as a negative part of the individual's personality. It is obvious therefore that one can and does make excuses but then this is done in excess, then it becomes a habit, a way of life and a person takes great pride in it thinking that other people do not know; it is then seen as a pattern of behaviour and people react to it. In the words of Benjamin Franklin, **"He that is good for making excuses is seldom good for anything else."** If one is perceived in this way, people will neither trust nor want to go along with the individual. People use excuses to shift blame or improve what others think about them but this may become more of a self-fulfilling prophecy than simply avoidance or laziness. The purpose of excuse is not to lose face with someone but when you are perceived as an excuse maker, the other person will throw your face away without your knowledge.

Ego protection is among the various factors that come in the way of relationships, and excuses are often times used to protect the ego. The examination question paper was set out of syllabus, the questions were so long, there was not sufficient time....work pressure, multi-tasking, ...these are all familiar words that are becoming easily dismissed even if it is borne out of genuine concern, for not coming up to the mark.

How many times have you used the phrase "in a meeting...will call you back" .... Were you really in a meeting and did you call back? How many times have you refused to answer your call because you know who is calling and probably assume that you know why the person is calling? What are you avoiding by such behaviour?

While looking at the effectiveness of excuses in protecting the self from the implications of failures and transgressions, the disadvantages of excuses have been relatively neglected. The triangle model of responsibility[43] provides a conceptual framework to analyze how excuses disengage the self from events and the conditions under which advantages and disadvantages accrue. On the disadvantage side, excuse-makers risk being seen as deceptive, self-absorbed, and ineffectual; they are viewed as unreliable social participants with flawed character. These undesired consequences result when excuses are used in ways that lower credibility (e.g., fail to receive corroboration), lower goodwill (e.g., blame failures on team members or others), and produce long-term disengagement (e.g., lead to failures to correct personal deficiencies). It is proposed that excuses are effective in the long run only if they balance short-term disengagement of the self and long-term engagement. Excuses are especially problematic when used to disengage the self from important, recurring tasks.

A spouse faithfully promises to take care of some household business, to be faithful, to do a favour or chore; the promise is not kept, excuses are given, and you are admonished for having expected them to fulfill the promise.

---

[43]Responsibility acts as a psychological adhesive that fastens an actor to an event and to relevant prescriptions that should govern conduct. People are held responsible to the extent that (a) a clear, well-defined set of prescriptions is applicable to an event (prescription-event link); (b) the actor is perceived to be bound by the prescriptions by virtue of his or her identity (prescription-identity link); and (c) the actor is connected to the event, especially by virtue of appearing to have personal control over it (identity-event link). Studies supported the model, showing that attributions of responsibility are a direct function of the combined strengths of the 3 linkages (Study 1) and that, when judging responsibility, people seek out information that is relevant to the linkages (Study 2). The model clarifies prior multiple meanings of responsibility and provides a coherent framework for understanding social judgment.

Psychol Rev. 1994 Oct; 101(4):632-52.

A grandchild promises to email or call parents on a weekly basis as a requirement to be complied with for taking up a job outside the town he lives with parents; but no call or letter is forthcoming, excuses are invariably made.

A contractor promises to complete a piece of work by a certain date; no one shows up to do the work, excuses are made.

A utility company says that a technician will show up at your home for a repair between the hours of 2 and 5 PM; at 7 PM you receive a call saying that the visit will have to be re-scheduled, excuses are made.

An invited guest to a wedding or dinner party RSVPs their intent to attend; without a phone call the guest simply does not show up.

Politicians make promises, in order to get voted into office; the promises are broken and excuses are offered.

We have all experienced one or more of these. It seldom feels good to be on the receiving end of a broken promise. When we express our displeasure, we are often told that we are uptight, rigid, controlling, have high expectations, etc. We are made to feel badly for having expected someone to honour their promise. Are we supposed to simply accept that this is the new way of the world?

What effect does having someone not deliver on a promise have on the relationship? For most people, the bond between them is weakened and trust is diminished. The relationship - whether with family members, friends, businesses, or government - is damaged. People fail to understand that integrity - doing what one says one would do - is an important aspect of creating trust. And trust is a vital aspect of intimacy. When we default on a promise we are in effect saying that the other person, who is counting on us, does not matter.

The depth of a relationship is defined in relation to the amount of value one claims for oneself relative to what one can reveal about oneself. It means that trust is about self-esteem. This is why in deep relationships, vulnerabilities of being taken for granted, being ignored, being ridiculed is not considered before one opens oneself to the other person in relationship. Trusting another, therefore, means that whatever value I claim for myself in interactions with that person will be understood and accepted, and the other person will not take advantage of me or use my revealed information to my disadvantage.

The constant use of excuses in relationship is the major cause for relationship breakages, be it intimate or non-intimate relationship. Trust is required for a person to actually share the truth that he has in mind. Sincerity, congruence, and trustworthiness reflect the degree to which one is perceived to be consistent across various roles and how much one's public face matches with one's inner values.[44]

Obviously, excuses foster lack of trust in any form of relationship. But how does this lack of trust affect relationships? Lack of trust causes anxiety, argument, decrease in self esteem, suspicion; these are detrimental to any form of relationship and often culminate in termination of the relationship. Lack of trust leads to partners avoiding each other, retaliation, and since the attention that is required in relationship is viewed with suspicion, self-esteem begins to diminish, even the truth begins to sound untruth, reasons become excuses, and reasons are questioned. In short, lack of trust severs any relationship and people have devised excuses to buttress their behaviours unmindful of the fact that the more excuses they use, the more the lack of trust prevails and persists.

Excuses actually don't change how the other person is feeling about being let down by you. Making excuses simply justifies your inaction to you. Excuses don't help you to make a better impression once you've broken your word. Everyone knows that if you'd really wanted to you'd have found a way to do it. Excuses don't actually excuse.

❑❑❑

---

[44]Edgar H. Schein, HELPING

Excuses and Personal Effectiveness

Hold yourself responsible for a higher standard than anyone else expects of you. Never excuse yourself

—Henry Ward Beecher

Excuses have the paradoxical quality of being widely condemned but widely employed. The psychology literature has articulated and provided evidence for the benefits of excuses, but the downside of excuses has been relatively neglected. We considered the disadvantages of excuses from the standpoint of their influence on character. Specifically, excuses are problematic when they raise questions about the actor's sincerity, causes the actor to disengage from valued goals, or suggest that the actor is self-absorbed to the pitch of disgust inasmuch as they disregard others and contravene rules of conduct.

Personal effectiveness is felt at maturity level.

[45]Journal of social and clinical psychology ISSN 0736-7236 2002, vol. 21

Self-disclosure - ability to state his/her "here-and-now" reality in the way he feels about it, rather than in garbs and pieces. It is the willingness to share one's state of mind resulting from an event, a situation or a given circumstance or behaviour.

Openness to feedback - while the willingness to share feeling is high, a person who is high on openness to feedback is willing to listen to the impact of his/her behaviour on others. The person does not necessarily wait for people to come forward to give him feedback but solicits the same from time to time. The person is open to listen out to all the impact his behaviour has on people before jumping into some form of action or the other.

Perceptiveness - ability to read between and behind lines. It is the ability to understand what is being said from what is not said. This demands more presence of mind to get in touch with self, question assumptions and clarify values. Nothing is left to conclusion without verification, and it is understood that perception might not be wrong but judgments based on it without verification can be wrong.

All of us have this ability to reach this high level of personal effectiveness and that is how we are but due to learning and experiences, we have deviated from what we originally are to what we are artificially made to be. How many of us are frank enough to own our own feelings no matter how ugly it is? How many of us are frank enough to tell the other person what he/she feels about that individual, work situation, relationship, etc.? We have become experts in excuses and thus lowering our self effectiveness, because we do not speak the truth any longer.

There are several reasons why we do not speak up either as an individual or as a group member but it is unfortunate that what we call "reasons" are mere "excuses" as we have been reading from this book. Such list of excuses, inter alia, is as follows:-

Its okay, I am fine (when actually is not okay nor are you fine)

It doesn't matter, I can manage (when actually it matters and you know that you cannot manage)

I am the newest member of the group I have not earned my voice at the table (when you are afraid of confrontation from an older member of the team)

I have no opinion about the issue (when you know that if you express your opinion, someone might give you extra assignment).

The fact here is that you have an opinion, you have a feeling, you have a perception but you hold it on to yourself, you are not able to express it to the group and, rather than admitting this inability, you tend to coat it with what appears to you as reasons but what others see as excuses.

The best way for us to have a positive impact on friends, family, co-workers, and our communities is to make sure our actions are strictly in conformity with our feelings. The most repeated motivational message, which is said thousands of times each day, takes place on every commercial airline flight as it is scheduled to embark upon: "In the unlikely event of loss of cabin pressure, be sure to put your mask on first and then assist those travelling with you."

We must be willing to take the steps that enable us to feel great about who we are and where we are going, in order to be able to help those that we care about. Our first step is to be aware of the choices we will make today. Our ability to manage ourselves through the many choices that will impact our attitude, energy level and personal effectiveness can be improved simply by developing an awareness of how we are choosing to live out each 24-hour block of time we are given.

Sometimes, it helps psychologically and emotionally to make up a phoney excuse for something. We may not want to reveal too much about ourselves (or a family member) to others, and will make up a phoney excuse. Other times we will make excuses to help us feel better about behaviours which we are trying to justify. The truth may be so embarrassing that we are unwilling to expose it to others.

But who says we must come completely clean anyway? Where's the harm in being playful with friends by making up stories? But, being a chronic excuse maker in the workplace or in your relationships is a whole other can of worms. Excuses generally are merely a ploy for shirking duties or avoiding unpleasant situations. Are your excuses getting in the way of leading a responsible life, attaining your goals, or securing that job promotion?

If you are someone who is a habitual excuse maker it might be a good idea to ask yourself why you deliberately choose to be less than truthful. Do you fear the scrutiny of friends, family, or co-workers? Are you uncomfortable with opening yourself up to others? Sometimes, making up a lame excuse to avoid attending a social event is done for self-preservation. Are you afraid your attendance would make you feel inadequate, vulnerable, or foolish?

Are your excuses meant to inflate your worthiness in the eyes of others? Ego does play a factor in habitual excuse making. However, indulging in ego-boosting through excuse making will likely to have the reverse result: deflated personal self-worth. You can trick others into believing a lie, but convincing yourself is not easy. Or is it? If you continue telling lie convincingly enough and keep getting away with it, you may also begin believing it yourself.

Excuses are meant to hide our shortcomings or give a better light to our failures. We can all justify our reasons for making excuses but how does it feel having been deceitful? Taking responsibility for your actions is the grown-up thing to do. Admitting your failures and accepting that you are not perfect may be hard to swallow at first. But that is the way of life and that is personal effectiveness.[46]

❑❑❑

[46]Are You a Chronic Excuse Maker? How to Change Deceptive Behaviors By Phylameana lila Desy,

Excuses and Decision Making

Decision making is part of life - in and out of work environment. Decision-makers are those who are responsible for making a judgment -sometimes crucial one - between two or more alternatives. Part of the leaders/manager's role includes having to make a series of large and small decisions. At the personal level reaching the right decision in every situation is an ambition that is well worth striving to achieve. Who is not a decision maker?

As I started writing this chapter, I started doubting how excuse can affect decision making. It is clear that a decision maker can use excuse to state why a decision is not made but if a decision is made, how does excuse impact it? One thing that came to my mind is that a decision maker is capable of making a decision that he/she knows is not the right decision but uses excuses to justify his decision. After all, decision-making is just another name for choice-making as both contain alternative ways and you need to choose one and leave the other. In other words, every instance that calls for decision making calls for choosing from alternative possibilities. This however, does not guarantee the success of the decision because things do and can go wrong at the end. What is important is that the alternatives come with 'hard' data that need be or are properly considered before a decision is taken.

We have a responsibility to make decisions at the personal as well as the professional level. Decision is the ultimate thing that needs be done. Action cannot commence unless decision is taken but decision can exist for years without action. We take decisions every day. In some situations, the decisions are readily taken and in others, deliberation takes longer before a decision is taken. The speed of decision making is dependent on the risk effect of a wrong decision, competing status of alternative actions, availability of data and personal bias. While the several factors can be verified, personal bias is difficult to verify especially when the decision maker has been swayed by selfish motive - recommending someone else for a reward or promotion rather than the deserving person. The decision maker has the whole gamut of excuses to justify this skewed decision and sometimes it is difficult to argue in favour of the victim.

A typical behaviour that I have noticed in many including me is that most of the suggestions given are things that we already know. For example, a person talks about feeling lazy or adding weight and if you suggest morning or evening walk, the response comes so sharply that the individual knows it. Even in collective decision making in the home or in the work place, observe that when others bring in good ideas or suggestions, the tendency of the leader to receive the input as a standard fact or to modify it for his own credit is high. This is because he/she does not want the others to take credit of the idea and it is defended in such a way that you will just give up your argument of biased decision, in spite of your conviction.

What is observed is that when the decision is made with proper consideration of the data available, one feels comfortable for the decision taken irrespective of what the end result would be. On the other hand, when a decision is made with insufficient consideration or manipulation of available data, the echo of the unmade choice keeps ringing in the ears of the decision maker. This echo is not a comfortable sound and is resented by the decision maker. In many instances, the decision maker is aware of his/her bias in making the choice but it does not end there.

Social psychology claims individuals experience cognitive dissonance whenever they make a decision, i.e. whenever one way of doing is chosen against another way of doing. It is to reduce this dissonance that the individual submits to a largely unconscious reduction of dissonance by creating new motives of the decision making that more positively reflect on self-concept. This process of reducing cognitive dissonance regarding decision-making relates back to the problem of individual becoming stagnant in a course of action. In order to alleviate this dissonance, he or she rationalizes their actions either by changing them, or in this case continuing on in their course of action, perpetuating their qualifying beliefs.[47]

One way of dealing with this dissonance is to invent several justifications to the action taken. It means that such justifications are not only excuses to which they are being provided to but a strong weapon in the hand of the decision maker to reconcile with the conflict escalation in his/her mind resulting from the decision.

It means that when decisions are made without proper consideration and weighing the options available, excuse serves to justify the inner conflict caused by this biased stance, though the excuse is provided as justification outside but consolation inside. On the other hand, when decision is delayed or not made due to the inability to choose from either of the options, it is also seen that the individual does not own up this inability but provides excuses as reason for delaying or not taking

[47]Staw, B. M. (1981). The escalation of commitment to a course of action. Academy of management Review, 6(4), 577-587

a decision. Many issues of procrastination emanate from this inability to make up one's mind and damn the consequence.

On many occasions, I have experienced myself using excuses to cover my laziness - be it in saying morning prayers or reading the Bible before getting up from bed, trying out stretching exercise as I have been thought and instructed, to taking the dog out for a morning work. I admit it is laziness but I have always found some other excuse in the form of reason to help me deal with this dissonance. At the professional level, I have also experienced several such situations where I am not able to take a decision as required but I console myself with excuses.

But life is just about making decisions. Every moment in life we are making decisions as our lives depend wholly on the decisions that we make. If the decision is good, you experience good life and if it is bad, you experience bad life. There is no other way that this relationship operates. It means that excuses are self-made or fictitious defences or justifications we provide without knowing how devastating the effect of it would impact our lives. Observe that only few of your excuses are based on reality and note that whenever you are true to yourself, excuses do not show up in any form.

Excuses can be used as a justification for a wrong decision or provided as a reason for non-decision. In either case, the decision maker has something to hide while presenting him/herself to the environment. It is wrong to assume that the other party is not aware of the role of bias in the decision making or how excuses are being offered as reasons for wrong or no decisions. Consider that many leaders are shocked with the ratings they get during their 360 degree feedback. It is possible that some of these leaders put up subtle behaviours and provide flimsy explanations in the hope that the aggrieved are convinced and believe them only to pay them back at this time of the year.

Nothing can be acted upon unless decision to do so has been taken. In other words, series of issues for action might line up but no action can be taken before a decision is taken. Consider, therefore, a leader who has all facts and figures about different issues on his table but delays in deciding which line of action is to be taken. What is the fate of his department, his position, the effectiveness of his team's performance and the overall image people have about him in the organisation.

Excuses and Responsibility

Responsibility is a duty or obligation to perform satisfactorily or complete a task (assigned by someone, or created by one's own promise or circumstances) that one must fulfill, and which has a consequential effect or penalty for failure.

I have taken 'being proactive', the first habit of Stephen Covey in his book, The Seven habits of Highly effective People to define 'responsibility' as it is used in this book. He advises "Look at the word responsibility - "response-ability" - the ability to choose your response. Highly proactive people recognize that responsibility. They do not blame circumstances, conditions, or conditioning for their behaviour. Their behaviour is a product of their own conscious choice, based on values, rather than a product of their conditions, based on feeling."[48]

---

[48]Read more: http://www.businessdictionary.com/definition/responsibility.html#ixzz2uC4QBz00

In the context of self development, responsibility, is the awareness and acknowledgment that one, through his thinking, feeling and behaving, is responsible for how he/she experiences life..., Jack Canfield Co-author of the Chicken Soup For The Soul series, writes in his book, The Success Principles, "It is time to stop looking outside yourself for the answers to why you haven't created the life and results you want, for it is you who creates the quality of the life you lead and the results you produce. You—no one else! To achieve major success in life, to achieve those things that are most important to you, you must assume 100% responsibility for your life. Nothing less will do."

In every moment, we are building our futures. And as Jack suggests, we have incredible control of what is being shaped for tomorrow. His formula is very simple:

The Event + Our Response = The Outcome

The sad thing about human mind and its meaning making process is that it is very deceitful and cleverly manipulates the individual.

There is no doubt that people are aware of their duty, obligation and responsibility, either self or professionally imposed. Living up to this responsibility is what is more challenging than mere knowledge of it. Accepting and implementing leads to responsibility accounting, while denial and rejection display one's act of irresponsibility. But who would like to do this? Yet we all do it.

Checking on why this can be so, I understand that there are :

i. ***Nature Imposed Responsibilities :*** family related responsibilities, such as looking after parents, wife, children, husband, etc.

ii. ***Professional Imposed Responsibilities :*** obligations and duties that fall on one as a result of the position one occupies in the organisation.

iii. ***Self-imposed Responsibility :*** what one expects from oneself, what others expect of him/her and what an individual does to belong and which activities might be out of his/her reach.

One of the things that I find common among people is that people misunderstand blaming someone else for not fulfilling one's own responsibility as a shift in responsibility. It is interesting to observe that responsibility cannot be shifted by simply denying it or blaming someone else without justification when the duty is not done.

I have also noticed that when I accept a responsibility, I feel good when I meet it up and feel bad when I fail to meet up with the obligation. Denial of responsibility and fault finding comes when I see the responsibility as a burden that comes in the way of doing what I want.

The field of applied behaviour that I work in has opened vast expanse of experiences why people deny responsibility. On several occasions, either upbringing, parental influence, others...are responsibility for one's lack of responsibility or something else is the reason for not living up to one's obligation. What is intriguing is the inability of the excuse maker to realize that when he/she points one finger on someone or something as responsible for non-fulfilment of an obligation, the rest three fingers point at the very person accusing another and the thumb finger looks embarrassed. It implies that what the other person or circumstance did to prevent performance or meeting obligation, you did the same thing three times more. Think about this.

Being responsible is the ability to make decisions and damn the consequences. It means that one has to look at one's ability to bear the consequences of a wrong decision before accepting a responsibility. It means that one has to understand one's own limitation to ensure that he/she has not bitten more than he/she can chew.

At the professional level, responsibility is given to the position, rather the individual as a result; positional responsibility does not vary with the individual but with the position. For example, the responsibility of a team leader remains the same for whoever assumes that position and does not discriminate age, sex or experience. This is the reason job description and responsibility accounting form part of the package that is handed over to the person assuming the new position. It is also important to note that the selectors consider a person's experience and ability to handle the prescribed responsibility of a position before recruiting or promoting the individual.

Excuses places the individual on a 'victimized' position in the workplace where things are let to happen rather than making them happen. This position often encourages defensiveness and helplessness and this can adversely affect other people who victimize themselves or those who feeds on the victimization of others.

Using excuses to exonerate one self from blame or to shift casual attribution to protect self image is an indication that one has not accepted the fallibility of man. It does not matter how smart we are, there is only so much responsibility that a person can handle. It is also important to remember that we are not responsible for things that are beyond our control, for example, how other people feel or how they react to us or to others. Accepting responsibility for both success and failure makes one more trustworthy and more responsive to responsibilities. The real meaning of responsibility is the ability to respond (response-ability).

Sometimes, the excuse used to shift the blame of not being responsible is an assumed excuse, a cast in concrete excuse. This is illustrated by the story of the baby elephant that was held with a small chain when it was small. Even as the elephant has grown big that it can push down branches and trees, yet elephant keepers proudly state that only strings can hold elephants at a place. This mentality is what is used when excuses are borne of perceived constraints or learned responses.

As Albert Ellis once said, *"The best years of your life are the ones in which you decide, your problems are your own. You do not blame them on your mother, the ecology, or the president. You realize that you control your own destiny"*.

Decidedly, in the present day economy, people's growth in organisation depends upon their response-ability to fast changing situations. One of the qualities being sought for, in putting people up, is the ability to handle demands, resources, projects, and tasks with competence and confidence. A desirable trait, in this connection, is the ability to take ownership of one's behaviour. Such traits create sense of trust, sense of reliability and people enjoy working with those who will share the glory and blame of good and bad decision respectively. On the other hand, not owning up responsibility can lead to regrettable consequences such as self hurt, interpersonal relationship and even the career part.

But, when you begin to take ownership of the things you think, say, and do, people will trust your ability to take on responsibility at work. This leads to real success. The more you embody responsibility, the more likely you will take on new challenges, and personal and professional growth. Furthermore, you will have more chances of attracting more positive support and be placed in leadership and management positions in the workplace.

Part-IV

Work Effect of Excuses

Work Effect

Fight or flight? This is the mantra (most common) reaction we give whenever we are faced with new challenges at work, or at the personal level. Obviously, behaviour is either to derive pleasure or to void pain; hence, the rewards attached to taking on a big new project, as also risks involved influence this initial reaction which, in turn, regulates our involvement in the task. We have been used to the default to focus on the risks and back away, citing excuses—different excuses. Yes, we can't take on every new opportunity, but we also can't endlessly pass on every opportunity.

As leaders in organisations and in our personal lives, it is important to note that our anxiety is easily passed on to those who are dependent upon us.

In this section, we will review how excuses affect not only personal effectiveness but also work effectiveness in relation to working with team, working as a leader and the impact of excuses on the overall performance and image of the organisation.

While it is natural to be scared with new and untried things, it is also necessary to filter to be able to distinguish the worthwhile pursuits from the mediocre diversions that are so common in our world of work. To create such a mechanism, one has to determine one's own non-negotiable - the things that cannot be sacrificed or compromised. These are the core tenets of one's circumstance and involve a deep dive into one's motivations. The result is clearer values and new perspective in regard to how to invest in one's work. The non-negotiable are a different ways of articulating limitations which no longer remain as limits but as guidelines to choose what to and what not to do.

Excuses and Team Work

We have more ability than will power,
and it is often an excuse to ourselves that
we imagine that things are impossible

—François de la Rochefoucauld

It can be challenging for a leader to have to deal with employees, who seem to complain about everything and anything. Any form of change initiative brings with it a chain-reaction from team members, because change is unsettling and takes one off one's comfort zone. There is, therefore, the human tendency to defend the old way of doing things rather than choose the new way. Change brings with it the fear of the unknown and as a discomforting situation for employees at least in the short run.

How are these fears presented in the group - as fears or as excuses? How do you distinguish between fear and excuse? Or are excuses accepted as legitimate tactics in your group? Excuses are destructive to collective efforts, irrespective of the nature of enterprise.

According to Daniel Flash, Excuses affect the worker-to-worker relationship as it kills trust, wastes time, delays solutions, ensures rework is required and blunts individual initiatives. A team that tolerates excuses legitimizes failure, creates a culture of blame, invalidates culture of responsibility, renders teamwork ineffective and fosters culture of cynicism.

Take the fear of the unknown and discomfort and what you usually get is excuses and some of them are so lame that you don't even think of any form of crutches that can make them stand. The manner in which the leader deals with employee resistance and excuses has great impact on team and the company's overall success.

Employees don't usually like being told what to do. Instead, they like to be included and feel validated. Ignoring excuses or forcing change without responding productively will have a negative impact on the team. Part of effective leadership is engaging team members in conversations about performance, concerns in achieving performance goals and the excuses that inevitably follow, as attempts are made to change or improve the way things are done. An obvious fact is the fear of the unknown which is inherent in human nature and this fear cannot be wished away nor allowed to prominently dominate the individual or the team.

The inherent resistance to change cannot be handled with clever or over-smart excuses as people are intelligent enough to know when they are not being told the truth. The fear of the unknown is responded to by providing knowledge of the future through proper communication skills and good interpersonal relationship.

Communicating what is happening, why it is happening, when it is going to happen, and how it is going to happen along with how it will impact the employees, customers, and the company is a good place to start. Communication is a key ingredient to get folks to change the way they are behaving or working currently.

It is through excuses that teams deny their responsibility, project blames on others, victimise others and externalise issues. It is through excuses that teams land into "self-deceit" and "helplessness" as well as "reactive" thinking. Obviously, any team in this circumstance will not function effectively.

It is important to notice how the company's projected plan (output, profit, expansion, etc) is responsible for excuses among team members. The Annual plans are made in hope of "all things being equal", but this is a rare phenomenon as the year progresses. As things change—market, product, people, etc., people are not able to meet their contracted obligation; hence, the tendency to protect themselves from blame and criticism. Excuse making is spontaneous and instantaneous to protect oneself from the emotional pain caused by the inability to deliver.

Observe also that a team that is full of excuses or complaints always looks for a scapegoat to project on. There is constant denial of responsibility, externalising issues by holding something or the other responsible. The object of excuses is always something or someone that is not physically present at the point of excuse to defend himself. This tendency to back-bite is never good for a group working together.

When people work together, they depend on each other to deliver and their collective effective delivery makes the work of the group or team effective. When things are not turning out as they are supposed to be, or when the team is not able to deliver, it is important to understand what the team presents as reason for non-performance - excuse or explanation. An explanation can let the team understand where things derailed and enable the team get back to track. This is because an explanation provides the reasons things happened the way they happened and not the way they were expected to happen. Everybody understands the reason and it becomes a learning point or a situation that has earmarked itself for observation.

When the inability to perform is offered as an excuse, people understand it because it is offered in the form of plea to exonerate oneself from a responsibility. Excuses do not provide correction points, because they present situations where the team cannot do anything to prevent it from happening. However, excuses undermine the efforts of the group to understand where corrective action is required.

Excuses and Leadership

Why do businesses fail? If you're willing to strip away all the excuses, explanations, rationalizations, and justifications for business failures, and be really honest in your analysis, you'll find only one plausible reason -poor leadership. FORBES

Leadership is about people and people alone. The quality of your organisation is determined by the quality of the people in the organisation. Leaders' role in shaping the organisational effectiveness is most essential. Leadership - leadership is about taking responsibility, not making excuses says Mitt Romney, a statement each one of us will not discard. Leadership is responsibility and responsibility contains 'response' 'ability' as well as can be used as 'responsiveness.'

A team depends on its leader for direction of purpose and pursuit of value while the leader depends upon the team for production of value and excellence. This inter-dependence is the key to effective team work and effective leadership. As will be discussed later, the principal building block and binding band of this inter-dependence between the leader and the team is 'trust'.

Leadership is about people believing that their leader is well intended, is transparent, is concerned and is responsive. Leadership is about people believing their leader. People believe their leader if the leader is consistent in explaining valid reasons which everybody finds inevitable. However, if the leader offers excuses, he/she looses credibility, because people know when they are told lies. Remember, that one of the ways for identifying a lie is to check if there are obvious alternatives.

Leaders neither offer, nor accept excuses. Leadership requires characters that demonstrate ownership for one's actions, and the courage to hold others accountable for theirs. Excuses on the other hand, attempt to conceal personal or professional insecurities, laziness, and/or lack of ability. They accomplish nothing but to distract, dilute, and deceive.

However, looking at the part of the leader, it is important to note that there are more excuses than reasons in today's world. The advance in technology which has made the world smaller has actually caused wider distance between people. One of the most common reasons I often hear these days is 'no network'. In a world where there is much to accomplish within time, there are professional and personal priorities, you either spend time in your work or in your house and not both...provide several implications for true leadership.

This is not to say that there are no true leaders. Everyone uses excuses at will and sometimes we even use it as a joke or to avoid causing pain to the other person. But as John Wooden puts it, "Never make excuses. Your friends won't accept them and your foes won't believe them."

Excuse is a sure route to leadership failure. No matter how alluring, "Difficulty is the excuse history never accepts." Edward R. Murrow. Effective leaders peel excuses from within, state the facts of the matter and damn the consequence. It is this ability that enables them to state the same to their subordinates, the need to be honest, transparent and not to use excuses.

Remember that you are no leader if you have no followers. One of the challenges I throw to leaders is to make a list of the several reasons why people leave their organisations. There is hardly any occasion where a participant mentioned his/her leadership as reason for attrition in the organisation. But they agree that leadership impacts retention and attrition in the company, may be, not their own.

I require that they make a list of reasons why their subordinates do not want to live them or why people should be led by them, I do not see the ability of not using excuses as one of the qualities.

People are branded by their behaviour. Consider a close friend, a college mate, colleague or social acquaintance who has the habit of providing excuses for everything. How do you feel about that individual in relations to continued relationship, working together or building closer relationship? This is so with your subordinates when they find out that you are make lots of excuses for reasons. Unfortunately, they will not tell you. As long as there will be reason for people not to follow you, there are also reasons why people will follow you. Principal among the reasons for not getting commitment from followers is when the leader is associated with excuses.

While working with leaders from a leading pharmaceutical company, I was initially attacked when I showed a presentation slide titled "people leave their leaders and not the organisation."

The embarrassment of this situation among a team that I am meeting for the first time made me become conscious of what could be the reason for this almost 'ready-made' attack. As we proceeded in the programme that lasted for about two and half years among different leaders from different places in the same company, certain facts became very clear:

- The ego structure of the popular and respected leaders is such that the more they shout at others, the more they show that they are sure even when they are not, the more recognition they will get.

- I struggled a lot to convince participants that 'leadership is character and not position', as a result, leadership is displayed in behaviour.
- Human behaviour includes falling short of expectations from time to time. This was agreed by everybody but as Kathryn Schulz, the author of "Being Wrong" puts it "As a culture, we haven't... mastered the basic skill of saying 'I was wrong.' This is a startling deficiency, given the simplicity of the phrase, the ubiquity of error, and the tremendous public service that acknowledging it could provide."

I refer to this pretended ignorance as Self-handicapping, which, according to Kolditz, T. A., & Arkin, R. M is the process by which people avoid effort in the hopes of keeping potential failure from hurting self-esteem. It was first theorized by Edward E. Jones and Steven Berglas, Rhodewalt, F., & Vohs, K. D. according to who self-handicaps are obstacles created, or claimed, by the individual in anticipation of failing performance.

In an article Forbes called Creative Leadership: Humility and Being Wrong. The authors, Doug Guthrie and Sudhir Venkatesh, make a crystal clear and well-reasoned case for the positive power of admitting and apologizing for one's mistakes. At one point in the article, they note that:

We are frequently taught that leaders, especially aspiring leaders, should hide their weaknesses and mistakes. This view is flawed. It is not only good to admit you are wrong when you are; but it can also be a powerful tool for leaders—actually increasing legitimacy and, when practised regularly, can help build a culture that actually increases solidarity, innovation, openness to change and many other positive features of organizational life.

The article continued to say that by embracing humility, creative leaders impart advantage to their organizations and themselves. Moreover, leaders must not only recognize their failures but also acknowledge them publicly. In being wrong, they can find both authenticity and opportunity.

❑❑❑

Trust - The Antidote to Excuses

"I'm not upset that you lied to me, I'm upset that from now on I can't believe you."
—Friedrich Nietzsche

In our rapport building before intervention exercise, we attempt finding out the specific activities that people do in their capacity as holders of the position. Along with this information, we require to know the behavioural requirements from others for performing such activities and how much of these are available.[51]

The gap between the requirements and their availability impacts what I describe as "The work before the work" The mutual effort needed to build effective communication and relationship; the team reality without which other tasks get done less efficiently and effectively—TRUST." There is always a 'can I rely on you' question in minds of people who work together, irrespective of how long they have worked together.

[51]This is used here for the purpose of illustrating the point in hand, and not for an elaborate discussion on behavioural requirements and what is available.

Hyler Bracey, Ph.D.[52] Defines TRUST as an acronym for :

Transparency

Responsiveness

Use care

Sincerity

Trustworthiness

Transparency

A lack of transparency results in distrust and a deep sense of insecurity.

—Dalai Lama

What is Transparency? How transparent are you by your definition of the word? Did you know that you betray yourself by your transparency, because you are not able to cover it up? Have you noticed that some of your responses come out of obligation, rather than voluntarily? Do you know that you have more 'care' than you use? What is the need for swearing to your sincerity if only you are sincere in your mind? Did you know that you trust only those who have proved their trustworthiness and that there are people you do not trust simply because they have not done so?

It is intriguing how the human mind works. How many times have you identified that people are giving

---

[52]Hyler Bracey, Building Trust. How to Get It! How to Keep It!

excuses, people are telling you lies, people are not honest, people have hidden agenda, what they are saying is not what they mean...? How did you know all these?

You know it because people are transparent. You can see through them by their body language, the shivering on their voice, the shakiness of their hands, the lack of flow in their words, the betrayal of their emotions. In the same way, you are transparent to others, so when you present excuse as reason, do not rejoice, because your own inherent transparency betrays you, tells the other person that you are not genuine in your statement. As already stated in this book, the other person will notice your inconsistency but choose to be silent for reasons best known to him. It means that everybody is transparent but this lack of self-awareness of the natural transparency is the bane of mankind. All efforts made to hide this tendency towards betrayal have always proven tough and unattainable.

Responsiveness

A leader is one who does not care about his rank and role but remains always responsive to lead, shoulder responsibility, and achieve the goal in such a way that everyone, in and outside the team, respects him for touching their revered souls.

—Anuj Somany Quotes & Sayings

One can be responsible but not responsive, and one can be responsive and not responsible. A responsible person is one who is in charge of or who is held accountable for particular action or outcome. This person is aware of this responsibility but may not be responsive to it. A responsive person is one who responds to situations, even as he/she may not be responsible ipso facto for the situation. Responsiveness in the sense used here implies a person who is accountable for, and answers or responds to, the situation as and when required.

Responsive persons rarely use excuses to abhor their responsibility, but use plausible reasons to explain why things are the way they are. They distinctly understand the difference between excuses and reasons - you can do something about excuses but you cannot do anything about reasons. Leaders who are not responsive are not trustworthy, because they can easily disassociate themselves from situations with their sharp wit in constructing excuses. Followers require leaders that would lead from the front so that they can follow and not leaders who would hide at the back of excuses. The great leaders of yester-years and current period never used excuses to express their inability but invariably and candidly admitted this inability, owned it up and that made all the difference.

Consider your relationships (personal, professional, social and otherwise), how satisfied are you with them. Is that what you are looking for? If your answer is no, what are your contributions in making the relationship the way they are today? Is there anywhere in your relationship or effectiveness that excuse is a concern? What are those things that hold you back from responding, and what excuses do you provide in such situations? People who are not responsive and people who are not responsible and responsive are not trusted.

Using Care

Leadership is solving problems. The day soldiers stop bringing you their problems is the day you have stopped leading them. They have either lost confidence that you can help or concluded you do not care. Either case is a failure of leadership.

—*Colin Powell*

One of the challenges of today's leaders is the ability to use care in dealing with the people they lead. I have always been made to believe that using care would make people complacent, take advantage of the leader, present the leader as weak... But is this always the case? The answer is no. What you are asked to do is to first determine what you want to achieve in the interaction or behaviour you want to put up. Once your goal is clear, how you will do it to give you what you want will automatically emerge. The major challenge in communication is that sometimes people do not know what they want at the end of their interaction.

Using care implies using care-frontation, rather than CONFRONTATION. When you use care-frontation, you are taking care of yourself and care of the other person. Remember there are certain things that you do as compulsions of your position which you would not ordinarily do. When you do those things, does the other person receive it from your professional or personal compulsions? This makes all the difference. People will trust you more when they know where you are operating from.

Using care means being more empathetic, and not more compromising, using care means more understanding and not more argumentative, using care means identifying common ground and not operating from different grounds, using care means being presence and not being present. Using care means, letting the other person know that you care.

Sincerity

To practice five things under all circumstances constitutes perfect virtue; these five are gravity, generosity of soul, sincerity, earnestness, and kindness.

—*Confucius*

Sincerity according to Wikipedia is the virtue of one who speaks truly about his or her own feelings, thoughts, and desires. Sincerity is the quality or condition of being sincere; genuineness, honest, and freedom from duplicity. Sincere expression carries risks to the speaker, since the ordinary screens used in everyday life are opened to the outside world. At the same time, we expect our friends, our lovers, our leaders "to be sincere". Sincerity implies 'the Truth and nothing other than the Truth'.

Sincere leaders are honest in every respect, they do not fake their feelings nor would they be insincere to others to gain favour.

Sincere leaders are up-front and the words of their mouth are the sword of their strength to conquer. They do not use burning hot words but firm in their statements because of their conviction that they are sincere beyond compare and calibration.

Sincere leaders manage their ego very well as they admit to their own inadequacies and ask for help where the need arises. They do not hesitate to seek clarification/ help from subordinates, they admit that they do not know when they really do not know.

Sincere leaders rarely start their statements with such phrases like 'to be sincere..' because they are sincere and nothing but sincere. They speak the truth irrespective of the risk they are exposed to, they stand for what is right irrespective of what others think, they are prepared to lose the bait, provided their sincerity is not compromised.

Sincere leaders are respected, trusted and have great followers in organisations. They do not use excuses to exonerate themselves but admit their inability to complete a task or when they are ill-equipped to take up a task.

Trustworthiness

The only way to make a man trustworthy is to trust him.

—Henry L. Stimson

You purchase groceries from the grocery shop near your house and remembered that you have not come down with your purse where you kept money and the shopkeeper asks you to go with your purchases and bring the money later. Another neighbour does the same thing but the shop keeper collects and keeps the material and asks him to go and bring money. What do you understand here? Who is trustworthy and why? Who is untrustworthy and why?

The shopkeeper has built trust on the two customers on the basis of consistent behaviour - you will always pay as you promised and the other person does not pay as per his commitment but comes back with lots of reasons (actually, excuses). Sometimes, he is not coming from home, sometimes, the key is not with him, just spend the money meant for the shopkeeper on something that urgently emerged. The first customer has proved his 'trustworthiness' and the other has not. You have to make yourself credible to achieve trustworthiness.

Trust is the belief that others have your best interest at heart. It is an unshakable reliance on integrity of a person. You cannot lead people who do not trust you but trust, like a building has to be constructed else the statement that 'trust in a person is broken' will have no meaning. Trust is not an overnight journey. Building trust takes time and varies from person to person in terms of building and in terms of the other person accepting what you offer as trustworthy. People trust each other in the belief that the other has their interest in mind and will not do anything to harm them for the fun of it or for any selfish gain. Trust is a belief that one would live up to one's promise or commitment; and, reciprocally, to live up to the expectations of the promises in terms of the promise given. Trust, again, is a belief one would act consistently in a given situation. Trust plays critical role in establishing and maintaining personal relationship and in one-on-one transaction.

As a leader, you commit to your subordinate that you will promote him to the next level if he performs consistently over a period of time but when the time comes you offer explanations (actually, excuses) why he was not promoted. Over a period of unfulfilled promises the worker starts losing his trust in you. The tragedy here is that the leader will never accept that he has messed up because there are so many other external things to blame unfulfilled promise. Three major factors that build leadership trust are as follows:-

Accountability

Some leaders work as though accountability, owning up or acceptance of shortcomings was not part of the leadership journey. Accountability is "being willing to answer ... for the outcomes resulting from your choices, behaviours, and actions." When the leader is accountable, it implies that he/she has taken ownership of those situations where he is involved. This makes the leader see to it that the work goes on as he wants to see it, and is willing to take responsibility if the work happens to be less than expected. There is no occasion for passing the judgment on others, pointing fingers, holding others responsible for what happened.

However, leaders who give excuses for the job that they supervise or for the people that they lead are, in other words shelving their responsibility and people do not trust anybody who does not take responsibility for his/her own actions. Accountability builds trusts within teams and organizations, because people know that they can depend upon each other. Leaders who are accountable for their actions and work are more likely to be trusted and respected, because people know that they will keep their word.

People admit their own mistakes, shares with others, seek help and get solution, because they are willing to be held accountable for their actions. Accountability singles a leader out for promotion because others have seen him as dependable and this is a quality of high potential leaders.

Integrity

A second important factor that helps build trust is 'integrity'. The Random House Dictionary defines integrity as 'adherence to moral and ethical principles, sound moral character and honesty. People trust leaders with integrity, as they become role models for them. Integrity is the hallmark of ethical leadership which includes personal responsibility. When a leader is said to have integrity, it means that the leader lives in accordance with his deepest values; is honest with everyone, and always keeps up his word. I define leadership integrity as doing what you say you will do. If you cannot do it, if it is not in your hand, do not commit to it, because your failure to do it will make you look out for excuses. Excuses are on the down side of integrity. People with integrity are humble have a high self-esteem, and are self-confident. It is with these characters that people with integrity take the risk of owning up and never deny their responsibilities by offering excuses.

Professionalism

According to the dictionary, professionalism means the conduct, aims, or qualities that characterize or mark a profession or a professional person whereas profession is a calling requiring specialised knowledge and often long and intensive academic preparation. It means that professionals have made deep personal commitment in developing and improving their skills as well as obtain necessary credentials that prove their efforts. The ethical requirements of certain professions consider it offence if a professional uses that profession to cheat others. It means that you have to hold the ethics of the profession, there is one and only one truth, and there cannot be two truths to a situation.

However, acquisition of certificates and degrees does not make one a complete professional, it is blended with the morals and ethos of that profession. In other words, professionals are highly respected because of their profound knowledge of their profession and would sound ridiculous if they use excuses to exonerate themselves from their responsibility. People who do not practise professionalism in the real sense of the word are hardly respected both at home and in the society.

According to Dave Bowman, a Human Resource Expert, "many experts agree that trust is perhaps the most important element of a harmonious, synergistic and efficient work environment. Organizations that have trust among employees are usually successful and those that don't frequently are not." He maintains that leaders will be trusted if the following criteria are satisfied:-

- They establish and maintain integrity
- Communicate vision and values
- Consider all employees as equal partners
- Do what is right, regardless of personal risk

On the other hand, people do not trust leaders who;

- Act and speak inconsistently
- Seek personal, rather than shared gain
- Withhold information
- Lie or tell half truths
- Are closed-minded

Commitment Vs Excuses

"The greatest thing is, at any moment,
to be willing to give up who we are, in order
to become all that we can be"

—Max Dupree

What is Commitment

I like the illustration given by Steve Pavlina[53] in his blog the explanation of 'commitment'. Without complicating the meaning, he simply writes:

"Put your head underwater and keep it there for a while. You'll soon realize that you're 100% committed to breathing. Notice that you don't make excuses not breathing. Notice that you don't worry about motivating yourself to breathe. Notice that you don't need to justify your desire to breathe. You just breathe. Commitment is **action**. No excuses. No debate. No lengthy analysis. No whining about how hard it is. No worrying about what others might think. No cowardly delays. Just go...."

---

[53]www.stevepavlina.com/blog/2011/10/**what-is-commitment**/

He lives readers with the challenging questions: "What if something gets in the way of your commitment? What would you do if someone tried to prevent you from breathing?"

When you commit, you pledge yourself to a certain purpose, an obligation or a line of conduct that is self-imposed and this is possible only when you believe in what you commit to. It means that the pre-requisite for effective commitment are strong belief in what you commit to. There is a saying that goes, "stand for something or you'll fall for anything." The next is religious adherence to those beliefs. Persistence with purpose could be the right description of commitment

Note in the above illustration that you have no excuse not to breathe and will not tolerate anything or anybody who would prevent you from breathing. The reason is that breathing is your livewire here and if you do not breathe, you will pass out. This is commitment.

Excuses come from lack of commitment. Commitment lives you no alternative than to perform what are committed to. As T.J. Thomson remarks:

"...the basic philosophy, spirit, and drive of an organization have far more to do with its relative achievements than do technological or economic resources, organizational structure, innovation, and timing. All these things weigh heavily in success. But they are, I think, transcended by how strongly the people in the organization believe in its basic precepts and how faithfully they carry them out." (From Thomas J. Watson, Jr., *A Business and its Beliefs - The ideas that helped build IBM*).

"There's a difference between interest and commitment. When you're interested in doing something, you do it only when it's convenient. When you're committed to something, you accept no excuses; only results."

—Kenneth Blanchard[54]

In June 2012 Balance, Success Tips, Christine Pilkington writes

"100% commitment is heaven. 99% commitment is hell. When you are not fully committed to something, there will always be a voice in your head holding you back.... When you commit fully to your business, you take action regardless of any negative thoughts that come up... You just do it.... With commitment, you don't need motivation or willpower. You just start taking action."

In my personal capacity, I have noticed that there are many things of interest and excitement that I would want to do. Sometimes these interests are strong, at other times they are weak. Sometime they stand out as the only thing to be done and sometimes they become secondary things to be done.

---

[54]http://thedalaillama.files.wordpress.com/2011/11/11-3-2011-1-55-37-pm.png

My interest in writing is like a child-hood dream. I have more than 50 drafts of different things I want to write on. Each will start well but in-between I still start finding reasons why I should not write

Who will buy and read your book

How can you compete with renowned writers?

Who will publish for you?

People will laugh at you for your bad writing

Just one of these thoughts is enough to let me abandon what I have been doing for last six months or so. It is now that I have realized that I was just interested and not committed. I was making excuses and convincing myself that I had genuine reasons. In recent times, I have seen myself in a different frame of mind, it is not that I have gotten answers to the questions that held me back from writing, but that I committed to putting my ideas down and this makes the whole difference.

However, it was not easy to commit to writing; I was consoled in my first book, because it was co-authored, even at that, I noticed that my fears were unfounded. It is when I started pushing past those excuses that an amazing inspiration to write started emerging. I now see the possibility of writing about anything and everything and I am willing to bring it out for others to read. I have become committed to my own belief and rigorously pursuing this dream. Looking back, I understand that for those things that I committed to do but which I did not do, I have ample reasons for not doing them. On the other hand, for those things that I am interested in and promised to do, but have not done hitherto, I have excuses for not doing them.

Denials and How to Handle Them

"The human mind isn't a terribly logical or consistent place. Most people, given the choice to face a hideous or terrifying truth or to conveniently avoid it, choose the convenience and peace of normality. That doesn't make them strong or weak people, or good or bad people. It just makes them people."

—Jim Butcher, Turn Coat

Consider such situations as when the group missed its deadline, targets are not achieved, attendance to meetings and events are poor, some departments work in silos, people talk about each other, rather than talking to each other. The realities of these situations are always truncated with excuses because people are not in position to take responsibility for their behaviour. However, as a leader, you need to be prepared to deal with different behaviours of people at different times. Sometimes it is smooth sailing, sometimes it is like sailing against the storms. It is important that you build trust so employees feel that they can come to you freely, treat employees as adults and not as infants, as mature people that matter to you, to the work in hand and to the organisation. Ensure that there are consequences to different actions. Such consequences should be either to deter or to nurture some select action. Timely intervention holds the key because 'delay is always dangerous.'

Admittedly, blunders will still happen, in spite of meticulous steps to prevent their occurrence. What do you do to get at the truth, rather than be provided with excuses which you have no means to prove except if you get the same excuse again (and if you remember that you got a precedence of that excuse on an earlier occasion). Does your action draw people to open up to you or does it scare people from talking to you? The question is why would anyone give you excuses while giving the clear picture to any other person? Is there anything about you that promotes this behaviour? Recall the last time your subordinate gave a reason for not doing a particular work. How did you respond/react to the honest confession? Did you call the subordinate back to appreciate the fact that he gave the reason for his not doing his work or did you shout him out for not doing the work (indeed for saying the truth)?

When an error has been committed, for example, when an employee comes with excuses for missing deadline, remember that the subordinate confidence is shaken and is not coming to you with any amount of joy and happiness on his face. It will help you understand this, rather than adding to the pain by shouting and name-calling. You are disappointed and you can convey your disappointment to the person concerned in a way that the person will understand your pain and commit not to allow that to happen again. If you explore the reason for the failure to deliver along with the concerned subordinate, it is possible that the entire reason for non-timely delivery does not rest on one reason or one person only.

Excuses for absents from work need be nipped in the bud before it becomes habit. Many people have taken to the habit of excusing themselves from work on Mondays and Fridays. Study has shown that most absenteeism happens on these two days either people want to start their weekend early or return to their work stations late by one day. Having a job means making a commitment, and when someone is absent or shows up late, it affects their entire team. If you supervise an employee excuses himself/herself for missing work or being late—even if that just means taking a long lunch break—you must respond quickly. If you allow someone to take advantage of the situation, it conveys that you are condoning their inactions or irregularities. As soon as you notice this, condemn and convey your approval or provide the necessary consequences immediately. This sends the message that absenteeism and late coming are non-tolerable behaviour in your department.

Everyone makes mistake and it pays if one notices the point where mistake has been made and feels the pain of the mistake. It is obvious that the same mistake will not repeat. However, if the team spends its time to find the culprit or if the person points finger to blame another person, there will be no end to it.

It is important to enable team members to understand the importance of asking for assistance when they need it, rather than moving ahead with insufficient information. Communicate that while mistakes happen, they can be corrected if they're caught early enough. Also, suggest that blaming others for their missteps creates unnecessary tension among team members. Remember, part of your role as a supervisor is to coach employees to greatness by creating an atmosphere that embraces open communication and trust in such a way, employees won't feel like they need to make excuses for their performances.

What About Me?

I am the only person in the world I should like to know thoroughly.

Oscar Wilde

A teacher walks into the class and children who were enjoying themselves in climbing on the chairs, writing on the board, imitating the teachers...suddenly become silent. The child, the subordinate in the work place tell everybody the truth of what happened and gives you the father/leader excuses about why things happened the way they happened.

In the above cases, both the teacher, the father or the leader may go around boasting how effective they are as they are feared, their presence make people walk out their pants. How true is this? The child is afraid of the stick the teacher has in hand and not the teacher, the child is afraid of losing the love of the father, rather than the father, and the subordinate is afraid of what the leader can do to his/her profession, rather than the leader per se. But how many of this people ever felt sad that people are not free to be themselves in their presence? This is another form of excuse where you rejoice that people are scared of you; as a result, they do not tell you the truth and, instead, face that sad side of you that scares people. The fact is that people do not trust you to tell you the truth. Rather than rejoice, it is advisable to check yourself as to why people are afraid to be open with you, to tell you the truth and nothing but the truth, why people give reasons to others and make excuses to you.

Trust is relationship and relationship is trust. It is important to maintain relationship with yourself, be in touch with yourself. This is how you do it:

Spend time with yourself and reflect on who you are

Understand yourself - increase yourself awareness

Communicate with, and listen to, yourself

Let your mistakes be your learning and turning points.

Respect yourself—values, interests, differences

Do not judge yourself much

Accept yourself as you are

Appreciate yourself

Be honest to yourself

Be willing to take risk

My brother-in-law's friend's father's grandmother's sister's aunt's turtle died, and yes, it was a tragic death. I simply cannot go into the details!

—Gary Busey's Excuses

Final Note

"There are thousand excuses for failure, but never a good reason."

—Mark Twain

My colleague was the first person to read a brief summary of this book. The summary is about two pages and her immediate question after reading the summary is...Sir, you have not told how to avoid excuses." So I am wondering how many of you readers that has this expectation to find solution to giving excuses after reading this book.

Excuses may appear very reasonable, but the truth is that, they are the reasons we give for failure.

Excuses are attempts to hide away:

— Inaction
— Weakness
— Lack of accomplishment
— Laziness
— Moral failure
— Poor conduct

What excuses do

Shift causal attribution away from self (it is not my fault)

Protect self-image (I am not the kind of person who would . . .)

Excuses that don't work (they make others feel angry and less respecting)

Internal (I could not find it)

Controllable (I ran out of time)

Intentional (I did not feel like going)

Excuses that work (they make people feel like they want to give you a break)

External (My mother wouldn't let me leave the house).

Uncontrollable (an earthquake knocked out the power).

Unintentional (I got into the wrong bus by mistake).

Why people are motivated to make excuses

Impression management

Want to impress someone significant

Gap between real and ideal or imagined self

The situation calls for it

The teacher/parent acts as the judge of good and bad excuses

An excuse could improve the outcome.

Self-image is put in jeopardy by threat

Fostering Responsibility to decrease excuse making

Teach cause and effect - help students learn that actions have consequences and we can grow both from our successes and failures.

Be consistent with your management and how you deliver consequences.

Build-up self-esteem (competence, belonging, and especially internal LOC).

Eliminate the need for students to make excuses - don't ask for them.

Eliminate the use of all blame. Blame is external and past oriented. Responsibility is based on an internal LOC and future oriented.

Do not accept any "victim language." Eliminate all learned helplessness.

Do not be the judge of good or bad excuses.

One of the major road maps to success and change is when we imbibe the mindset of refusing to embrace, accommodate, and tolerate excuses. I will continue to emphasise the fact that it is not possible for me to provide a standard prescription or steps in avoiding excuses. The reason is that I understand that every disease has a cause and the same disease might have different effect on different people, and there is no way of asserting that the same prescription will work for the same disease in different people. This is the case with excuses. Excuse is Excuse irrespective of who gives it and/or where it occurs but the reason for choosing to make excuses will vary from individual to individual.

In the context of our modern way of living and the challenges it poses excuses have become part of our daily life as our "to-do" list becomes more and more or an endless checklist. What we really want to accomplish—such as better health or balance, good relationship and neighbourhood—keeps dropping to the bottom while our perceived "have-to's" rise to the top. This has become a vicious circle that just adds to our excuses—we don't achieve our goals because we have too much to do and not enough time to do it so we make more excuses; then we feel bad and eventually we just surrender.

But remove the word "excuse" from your personal vocabulary and treat it as though it did not exist and is a taboo. You will see how active, proficient, successful and accomplished you will be. Excuse is a self-defeating habit that can be handled or tackled only when we stop pushing ourselves. If this is done, it is possible to get perspectives that will surely confirm that we are even doing more than we think or know that we are doing. Stopping to push ourselves enables us to be able to hear the message of our body—headaches, backaches, frequent colds, and anxious moments—that require our attention. Stopping to push ourselves will enable us to learn to say "no" to requests that we cannot accomplish and to resist a culture that dictates not only what has to be done but how it is to be done also. Excuses are so cheap that unsuccessful people can afford so much of it - it is just a dime for a dozen.

"One thing we all need to remember is that a little effort is the best replacement for excuses."

—Donald Trump

DON'T EXPLAIN EXCUSES, EXPEL THEM TO EXCEL! EXPEL EXCUSES AND RESPECT COMMITMENT!

THAT IS THE WAY FORWARD.

Tips for Reducing Excuses

There may be similarity in the pattern of excuses that people give as reason for doing or not doing; however, I believe that even as the pattern or the excuse culprit such as 'time, traffic, others....' Is the same, the reasons for excuse differs from person to person. In this connection, it sounds generic to offer suggestions to handling excuses but let me try to give you a perspective that might help you decide to continue or to discontinue using excuses.

Observe that there is a prompt to behaviour. Observe also that the way of expressing the behaviour is either to derive pleasure or to avoid pain. In other words, to start the work on reducing excuses or even eliminating their use, it is important to reflect and understand the prompt and whether the excuse is made to derive pleasure or to avoid pain. Whatever is the purpose of the excuse, there is a price that is paid and whether the person making the excuse is aware of the price he/she is paying for what he/she is doing is a question that the individual alone can answer.

The journey of change is not as smooth but one who decides to make a change must follow that painful route to emerge victorious.

Let us look at the reasons why people use excuses once again and go through the tips that can help in handling similar situation with less or no excuses.

Situation I - *Getting out of personal responsibility because of fear of getting into trouble or the punishment it brings about*

You witness a murder, robbery, rape or any heinous crime but deny knowledge of anything about it, for fear of getting into trouble or facing reprisal. How many of you have succeeded in this type of situation, very few if any. The reason is that who is going to ask you has a reason for asking. Somewhere you are seen in the picture.

You are already in the picture, the more you deny your knowledge, the deeper you get into the trouble that you are avoiding. Just say what you know and that is all that is asked of you.

What is at risk that can survive only in lies and excuses? If it would land you in trouble, it does not matter whether you give excuse or own responsibility.

Situation II - *Hiding fault, insecurity and Incompetence*

You pretend to know when you really do not know, you goof it up but hide under excuses, you are incompetent for the assignment but you feel threatened by insecurity.

Consider the benefit of owning up your ignorance. When would people come forward to help? Is it when you claim that you know or when you admit that you do not know? In my case, the later is my reality.

Would you feel secured under a false roof? In the same way, giving excuses for threat of losing position is more disastrous.

Do you have any experience of having been rejected because you owned up a responsibility? Ponder over this question before you take up a stand as most people experience belongingness when they own up their responsibility.

Situation III - *Protect our interest, as truth hurts*

When it is said that 'truth is bitter', sometimes I wonder who finds it bitter. Is it the person who said the truth or the person to whom it is said? Excuses are made to hide the truth and when the person to whom the excuse is given is not aware of it, how can't it taste bitter to him/her. In other words, truth is bitter to the person who said it because it exposes him/her.

Think of the possibility of protecting your interest by faking the truth. What would happen to your interest when the truth is revealed?

Impersonation is an offence punishable by law. You give excuse to a person you know or perceive is above you, just as the law is above every citizen. If the person comes to know, you do not only lose your credibility but also your interest which you want to protect.

Excuses will exclude you from the ownership of your interest while truth will make you a strong contender for your interest. It is advisable to present proper credentials to claim your rights and by excuses, you are just doing the opposite.

Situation IV - *Justification for our doing*

Everybody wants to be seen as without blemish even if the person carries an indelible stain of character. You cannot give an excuse for what you are helpless about but for what you can but you have not done. It is better to say the reason why it is not done rather than giving excuses and spending more energy in wanting to justify the excuse. To do this, you need more and more excuses because you cannot justify excuse with reason.

A woman can excuse her protruding stomach at the most, for the first three months of pregnancy with having eaten much, gastric problem...after three months, what are the other options available to her as she would not accept that she has tumour in the stomach.

Notice that when you give an excuse, you need another excuse to justify the first one , another to justify the second and so on. How many excuses would you have to justify one excuse for more than twice?

Remember that the other person to whom the excuse is being made to is also intelligent and can read between the lines, even if the person does not attempt to disprove or argue with you. When you think you have won, the fact is that you have actually lost in integrity and trust.

Situation V - *Avoid feeling of shame*

What is shame in your definition? Consider how presenting an inanimate object as reason for your not living up to expectation would exonerate you from shame. What would make you comfortable? Is it when people change topic of their discussion when you come closer to them or when they continue to discuss their topic even when you are there?

Owning up holds the key to personal effectiveness, the fact that one is not able to complete a task does not mean that one does not want to do. The saying goes that "man proposes and God disposes", you may be keen on doing something but for some reason you are not able to do it. The best would be to acknowledge the unforeseen circumstance that caused you not to do it, rather than giving excuses.

Shame is a state of mind that one falls into when one experiences a sense of guilt even when nobody is holding you guilty. It is more when one does not live up to others expectations. Shame will disappear the moment one realises whose expectation is more important - my or others expectations on me.

Situation VI - *Inability to face reality*

'Honesty pays'. What man are you if you cannot face the reality of your situation? Reality is the state of things as they really exist and not as they are supposed to be. When you give excuse, it is associated with that which is not real and you know that what you are saying is not real. It is you who has to deal with the dilemma of not stating things as they are. The receiver may believe you completely as he or she has no way of proving you wrong. But does your conscience live you free? The answer is 'no'.

Man has learnt to put out all that are supposed to stay in and by so doing, has deprived himself of the ability to confront self. There is too much of self denial. If you would stop and check what happens to you when you distort the truth with excuse, you will note that the feeling is not good. Until you are able to experience this feeling of 'bad' when you give an excuses, you will continue to put the enjoy this momentary relief. Behaviour is either to derive pleasure or to avoid pain. When you give excuse, you derive momentary pleasure but expose yourself to prolonged pain of the conscience.

Situation VII - *Protecting our loved ones*

People seldom do what they believe in. They do what is convenient, and then repent. (Bob Dylan). But there's more to it than repentance, including: distraction, forgetting, trivialization, self-affirmation and denial of responsibility to name a few. These are easily granted by the individual when it comes to protecting loved ones. Who said that 'reasons' will break love and 'excuses' will protect it. Who would you call your intimate friend? The person who gives excuses or the one who tells you the reason for not living up to your expectation? It has been mentioned earlier that you cannot hide what is not true for a long time. Imagine a situation where you are giving excuses to protect your loved one and he/she finds out that you are just making excuses. How would you feel?

❑❑❑

Comments by Readers

The book was truly a great work of your insight and experiences of human behaviour and held a mirror in front of me to see myself and some of my close friends whom, I believe, I know, but find it difficult to explain their behaviour at times. Really could connect with book and the chapter on Excuses and relationship was revealing.

The final note is bold and showed your acceptance of the feedback and, at the same time, the conviction of a human behaviour facilitator to follow religiously.

Excuses often do not allow us to take the ownership of failures and at times success (for people who are low on self confidence). Excuse has a direct correlation with disowning. I give excuses in workplace to disown failure like "Boss you only have asked me to do it this way...." where I pretend to forget that I am supposed to review the expected outcomes and make course correction or I am supposed to own up the quality of the plan that is getting implemented. This leads to conflict, arguments which affect the quality of the professional relationship.

In personal life we often do not own up and hide behind the excuse of " You know I am like this, I told you before ..." or "I do not know what happens to me in presence of that person". This disappoints the person who is listening to this and often puts him/her into a spiral where they start questioning "whether they are into a relationship with the right person"

I very strongly believe that this book will go a long way to sensitize many of us and put us back in the right track.

Suva Chattopadhyay
General Manager, Sales Excellence
Abbott Truecare Pharma Pvt Ltd
Mumbai

Most people often attribute success to personal factors, but failure is often attributed to external factors, beyond ones' control. The book "Excuses" presents a mirror on an every-day activity we all indulge in at some point in time - making excuses for failures or commitments not fulfilled. The book propounds "reasons" for why we do so, and the impact it has on our thoughts, feelings and behaviours.

The author has used his knowledge of psychology and behavioural science to delve into the unconscious processes of human behaviour, in the context of excuses. The author offers no simplistic solutions of how to avoid the habit of making excuses; he only offers how liberating is the process of being able to get rid of it. Only when we are rid of the habit, will we be able to be, as Shakespeare put "to thine own self, be true".

Archana Sharma, Ph.D.
Faculty, IBS, Mumbai

I thoroughly enjoyed reading the book. It is a very hard hitting book that will shake you up and make you think. I can relate to the book very well, because as the book mentions, excuses have almost become a way of life for most of us. This book helps us understand why we make excuses and how excuses impact almost every area of our life. Once reading is not enough, we must keep on reading this book from time to time to get out of the excuse-making mode!!!

Shirley Iyaz
Unit Head,
Software Paradigm Infotech Pvt. Ltd
SPICITY
Mysore

" I am not surprised, with the depth of Experience that Zeb has in understanding Human Behaviour to come with a topic like Excuse. It has helped me understand that, Excuse stands between Success and Failure, one can easily chose to avoid these subtle nuances on our day to day functioning and chose to be euphoric of this precious thing called LIFE !!!. ?.

Soomanna MM
Human Resources,
Kotak Mahindra Bank Limited,
Bangalore

This book has been researched with admirable thoroughness and interest....I was completely taken aback by the spectrum of excuses and the reasons behind them, and, I have to admit, I am guilty of using some of the reasons for excuses I! The use of pithy quotes at the beginning of each chapter help to keep the reader interested in the book, like proper seasoning being sprinkled on a dish.

Meenu Vadera
'Founder - Director Sakha Consulting Wings Pvt. Ltd.' - New Delhi
'Founder - Director Azad Foundation', New Delhi

It was very interesting to read this book as it explains in detail how we human beings hide behind excuses rather than daring to stand up for our actions or inactions under various circumstances in our lives be it in our personal, family, or professional settings. I was told that only if we own up our actions can we cleanse our soul and grow and needless to explain, excuses will only stop us from that.

Syed Sohail Perveez
Marketing Head
108 Emergency Services
GVK EMRI, Bangalore

As a youngster I am looking for great achievement in life but my past 13 years of work experience. I found lots of 'but' and 'if' in each steps. Experience of 'excuses' is a great journey and this experience provided answer to most of my questions and challenges and also help me overcome the same.

Now I am able to understand the difference between excuses and reason and this helps me to perform and through this I can make a change in my way of doing things. This also helps me use it a tool. While discussing with my friends felt that issues related to personal effectiveness, relationship, emotions and teamwork can make easy to deal. Statement mentioned in each chapter is more punching and effective and provide the essence of the text.

CHECK THE SELF MIRROR ARTICLE IN BOOKS 2012

THE WHEEL OF EXCELLENCE IN PERSONAL EFFECTIVENESS

RN.Kumar Faculty (Behavioural Science) Administrative Training Institute, Lalitha Mahal Road, Mysore- 570011

❑❑❑